Dirt and Dust

A TEENAGE PERSPECTIVE ON LIFE AFTER THE SUICIDE OF A PARENT

AMELIA OLSEN with **RILEY OLSEN**

First published by Ultimate World Publishing 2021
Copyright © 2021 Amelia Olsen with Riley Olsen

ISBN

Paperback: 978-1-922597-55-7
Ebook: 978-1-922597-56-4

Amelia Olsen with Riley Olsen have asserted their rights under the Copyright, Designs and Patents Act 1988 to be identified as the authors' of this work. The information in this book is based on the authors experiences and opinions. The publisher specifically disclaims responsibility for any adverse consequences which may result from use of the information contained herein. Permission to use information has been sought by the authors. Any breaches will be rectified in further editions of the book.

All rights reserved. No part of this publication may be reproduced, stored in or introduced into a retrieval system, or transmitted in any form, or by any means (electronic, mechanical, photocopying, recording or otherwise) without the prior written permission of the authors. Any person who does any unauthorised act in relation to this publication may be liable to criminal prosecution and civil claims for damages. Enquiries should be made through the publisher.

Cover design: Ultimate World Publishing
Layout and typesetting: Ultimate World Publishing
Editor: Victoria Pickens

Ultimate World Publishing
Diamond Creek,
Victoria Australia 3089
www.writeabook.com.au

Dedication

Keep the sun on your back,

Love from us xxx

Contents

Dedication	3
Introduction	7
CHAPTER 1: You & Me	11
CHAPTER 2: WHY?	25
CHAPTER 3: Week-Long Therapy Group for Men!	41
CHAPTER 4: Motorbike Meditation	49
CHAPTER 5: Old Bull vs Young Bull	63
CHAPTER 6: Don't Overthink, Just Ride!	77
CHAPTER 7: Unicorn	91
CHAPTER 8: Wingman	101
CHAPTER 9: Flowers Can't Fix That	113
CHAPTER 10: Knots in Jocks!	125
CHAPTER 11: Top!	141
About the author	155
Acknowledgements	157

Introduction

Suicide.

There, I said it.

It's confronting. It's conflicting. It's confusing.

When I was fifteen my dad died by suicide. To be honest, it was a complete and utter shit-show. But somehow, after tragedy, the rest of us didn't get a choice; we had to go forward, no matter what.

Mum: *I think I need to write a book for young men about what happened with your dad.*

Me: *Mum, boys don't read books.*

Mum: *Well, I hope they read this one.*

Me: *Why?*

Mum: *They might learn something.*

Me: *Learn about what?*

Mum: *The hole that's left after someone takes their own life. How the rest of us question everything, forever. Maybe people need the heads up about a few things in this lifetime…*

Me: *Jeez, Mum, don't hold back!*

Mum: *Someone's gotta say it…might as well be me!*

Me: *Why do you always think you have to do the dirty work? What if people want to find out for themselves?*

Mum: *Yeah, but what if they have questions and no one to freakin' ask? Do me a favour… this is your story, too; you're an eighteen-year-old young man, just read it and tell me what's missing.*

And that was how eighteen-year-old me ended up with the job of narrating our family's version of the events around my dad dying.

For the purpose of telling a concise version of this story, there is almost seven years' worth of conversations condensed into seven characters, and the story is told over seven days. This book is not a fairy tale. It comes with both a language and content warning. To say the least, the act of taking a person's life by their own hand is dreadful. Depending on your experience and your perspective, you may find our story offensive, confronting, or contradicting to your own experiences and beliefs. Or, if you know us, it could be the story you thought it would be. But please understand, every circumstance around suicide is different.

Introduction

In Mum and Dad's twenty year shared time span, there are three main parts to what happened. There was about fifteen years spent in 'love and save' mode, eight months of 'hoping that everything was okay' when Dad was without us and there was no communication from him, and then after he died; the grappling to 'accept an adult decision' for us.

That last part goes on forever.

The toughest conversations are about being honest regarding mental health and the impact it has on those around them.

It's no one's fault, and it didn't have to be like this. We wish it was different, but it's not.

If suicide ever crosses your mind in the future, please reconsider. It is understandable that at times people feel empty, lonely, abandoned, rejected, worthless, or dead set fucking crazy, but you have to try everything possible to stay alive. More than likely, you have a life that other people would be envious of. Please get the help you need because you are loved, and the fall out for everyone else is horrendous.

When people are suicidal, we can only empathise that they are saturated with depression or are irrationally anxious. It is important that when everything is going okay to identify what that feels like. Photograph that feeling in your heart and mind. Save it, so you can conjure that image up later, when you need to flip your thoughts from negative to positive.

The toughest times in life are transitions—all of the unknowns, disappointments, making decisions, recreating your own identity, repackaging your purpose. It's all of that stuff no one knows how it will turn out until you actually do it. And maybe life isn't about what you have, but what you don't have that makes you a better person. You see the gap and fill it with goodness. Understanding that somehow you have to believe there is power in the rebuild, you just have to be brave enough to face it. I know that the answer to difficult life stuff doesn't have to be death. Just like the snake metaphor used throughout this book, we hope that by the time you read this, each of us have shed our skin and grown into a new one.

If you have ever been suicidal—and in our attempt to understand what it's like as the family standing, peering deep into that black hole, yet left behind—we apologise if we have misunderstood what it truly is like. But ultimately, that is also the privilege of being naive enough not to know or completely comprehend that death is a better option than life.

Sharing this story has been a difficult balance between telling the kick arse truth and being gentle enough to survive each of our own individual lives, and our choices from here on into the future. Because although this story is about the ride to Cape York based on Mum and me, there are three of us in our little family. There are three of us who still have so much life to live and love to give.

My sister is actually the anomaly in all of this, because she was Dad's girl. It hurts like hell to expose our souls on such a sensitive topic, but if it helps someone else, if it brings a level of understanding or insight because you need it, please take it. You're welcome, and we want you to have it.

With love, from the three of us xxx

CHAPTER 1

You & Me

"Fuck it, Mum, we'll go! You and me…"

It was another Saturday morning. It felt like it was raining inside our house just as much as it was raining outside. Mum had tears streaming down her face again. There was only one thing left on the bucket list Mum and Dad planned. We didn't intentionally carry out the dreams, but one at a time they presented themselves and this was the last one.

After six years' worth of training, a daydream was about to become reality. It had been nearly three years since Dad took his own life. The drain of disappointment after someone's suicide is dreadful. Yet here we were, finally on our way…

Destination: Cape York, Queensland. The last frontier. The pinnacle of adventure motorbike riding in Australia.

Announcements echoed through the airport; loud, yet crisp and crackly. I imagined the airhostess's spit spraying on the handheld microphone. It exaggerated the hissing sounds in her speech before she clunked the receiver down on the bench at the end of her message. Chaotic humans, completely unaware of what was going on around them, stopped to look at the 'arrival' and 'departure' screens. My eyes were able to drift across the range of busy people scattered here and there, and I thought about how there were lots of advantages to being tall.

Strangers always looked up at me, and then down at Mum. They usually said something like, 'Jeez, you must get your height from your dad!' I can only ever be gracious when that happens. I would smile and nod, no words necessary. It was like stating the obvious. Mum was on the small side of average and my sister and I were both long and lean, like Dad. I'd only just finished high school and a little bit of blonde facial hair had started to erase my boy look, but nothing other than Dad dying made me feel like a man yet.

The airport escalator chugged upwards to the next floor. Mum, who stood in front of me, turned and smiled an anxious but excited smile. We both wore backpacks and had large, matching carry bags resting at our feet. Hopefully they contained everything we needed for a week. It was too late now if they didn't!

After boarding our plane to Cairns, it wasn't long before Mum and I collected our baggage from the loaded carousel. It surged under the weight of a mishmash of suitcases and bags of all shapes and sizes, slithering like a reticulated python in the arrival section of the terminal. I thought about how grief made me feel like a carpet snake, one that had swallowed a giant wombat so big it dislocated my jaw. With time, the wombat kind of worked its way down, but something would happen—a reminder, a conversation, a memory—and the wombat would come straight back up and get stuck in my gut again, not going anywhere.

Tourists were keen to grab their luggage and go, that excited buzz of wanting to hurry on to their holiday destination. Our bags were big and heavy, filled with the lumps and bumps that included boots, helmet, jacket, knee guards… the usual stuff when you were about to be a crash test dummy on the back of a motorbike for a week. Mum was pretending not to struggle with the awkwardness of her bag, so I casually walked past and scooped hers up in my left hand—I justified that it was easier for me to be balanced with two bags. She smiled a 'thank you' at me and trotted along behind.

The tropical humidity instantly sapped our energy as we made our way to the taxicab rank. A driver with an accent asked Mum, "Where you wanna go, lady?" And after a short ride, we were delivered to our location. We stood outside a shed with a dozen brand new, bright yellow motorbikes lined up, ready to meet our tour guide and fellow riders for the adventure of a lifetime!

Mum had spent months brainwashing herself, watching YouTube videos of this ride, convincing herself she could do it. As we sat on camping chairs inside the shed a wave of anxiety and doubt came over me. I thought, *bloody hell, Mum, we are beginners at this!* Here was me, wearing shorts and thongs, with my little mum sitting beside me smiling at the rider briefing in her summer dress and sandals. All of the other riders were blokes with their big boy sons. *What the hell are we doing?*

Gus introduced himself. He was a short, stout fella with a voice to match. I'm not sure if he really had dark hair and olive skin, or whether that was the result of taking tour groups to Cape York for nearly thirty years.

With the assistance of one of the younger tour guides, Gus was demonstrating how to carry our motorbikes through water crossings. My eyes were wide. *Fuck*. I'd never had to actually pick a motorbike up like that, let alone carry it through water. How much water were they expecting? Seriously!

Gus's cigarette-smoker, chainsaw voice continued, "One man needs to be on either side of the bike. Hand on handlebars and the other hand to lift the bike by the foot peg, like this…"

I secretly compared Mum and I to the other pairs or trios that were about to ride. *Jeez, if this was a survivor type challenge, somehow, we're the weakest link. We are the two least experienced riders here, and Mum isn't going to be able to do that!*

I'd only had my licence for three months. And Mum, well, she gave up training on the motorbike six weeks ago in case she hurt herself. She'd already had a couple of big stacks. And in a practice run, the local cop followed her down the Black Snake Range one afternoon in what he referred to as his slowest police chase ever. In her own defence, Mum laughed with the policeman and said she couldn't pull over because there was nowhere flat for her to stop without dropping the bike because she was only just balancing on her tippy toes. She'd already dumped the bike once and broke the rear vision mirror off, so she didn't know the policeman was chasing her. He slapped her on the back and told her to go straight home because it was nearly dark, sending her on her way.

That was my bloody mum! I really wasn't sure we were going to be capable of this big ride. I fairdinkum thought she might have bitten off more than either of us could chew this time!

I snuck a sideways look at Mum listening intently to every word of advice being blurted out by our tour guides. She sat there nodding and smiling in acknowledgement. My heart was banging so loud in my chest I didn't hear a word they said. Meanwhile, Mum looked totally oblivious to the extreme level of danger we were about to endure. I'm not exaggerating here; seriously, why would anyone let two nut-cases like us out on a fourteen-hundred-kilometre ride in the middle of nowhere? Maybe that was why they made people sign an indemnity, a waiver? So, if you were crazy enough to do it, the risk and responsibility was all on you.

Gus continued to broadcast the safety messages loud and clear. "Just remember, this is a tour, not a race!" Then he added, "We'll all get to the same destination whether you go fast or slow." Gus looked over at Mum and I as if to say 'this is your last chance to pull out.' Neither of us flinched. Then he announced, "Righto you blokes, get your gear on!"

The men headed back to their bags that were waiting on the lawn and whipped their casual clothes off in broad daylight. Meanwhile, Mum snuck into the shed and hid behind a boat to get changed. We were all assigned a bike for the week, each with its own number on it. I was getting acquainted with my Number 12 bike when Mum came out of the shed. The bloke on the bike next to me spoke to her with an element of surprise, with one eyebrow cocked in her direction. "Are you riding?" he quizzically asked.

Mum beamed one of her famous, undefeatable smiles in return. "Yeah," she said as she looked at her boots and held her arms open, helmet in one hand like a professional. She replied to him in a matter-of-fact voice with a nod, "Looks like it!" She gave me a quick wink then walked to the end of the line and hopped on the bike that had been lowered to cater for her short legs. With a bit of luck, she could pull over the next time a policeman chased her because firstly, this bike hadn't had the mirrors smashed off yet, and secondly, her feet could actually touch the ground.

But before we could get going, a man I hadn't previously seen appeared with his mobile phone in his hand. He was talking and taking long strides towards Mum. Just as she was tying her hair into a stumpy, low ponytail and about to put her helmet on, he said, "You must be Amy?" She smiled and nodded. He said, "I've got Skye on the phone for you."

"Skye?" Mum questioned whether she even knew anyone by that name. She reluctantly took the phone from the man, "Amy speaking…" That was her teacher voice, the one she used when she wasn't sure what was going to come next. It had just enough kindness in her tone, but also said 'don't muck with me either.'

I could hear the bubbly female voice on the other end of the phone from where I sat a few bikes away. "Amy, it's Skye! Skye from Ag College in Victoria, from like twenty years ago!" The female speaker paused and waited for Mum to register who she was talking to.

A face of recognition and an enormous smile came over Mum's face. "Oh, my goodness! Skye! How are you? How did you know I was here?"

Why do women do that? Why does the pitch of their voice go up a couple of octaves when they squeal in delight? Bubbly voice Skye, a weird phone call stranger a minute ago, threw my forty-year-old mum into teenage girl mode.

Skye continued, "I can't believe it! I just saw your Facebook status about riding to the cape. Chooky is my next-door neighbour!"

"Umm… who is Chooky?" Mum asked.

"He's the cook on your trip. He doubles as the truck driver!"

Mum looked around for the man who handed her the phone. He was throwing our bags and a whole stack of camping gear into the back of a truck. As I looked at him, I supposed he did have legs that looked like an oversized chicken.

Skye kept talking, "Oh my God, you crazy woman, you haven't changed in twenty freakin' years!"

With that, I wondered how crazy my mum was twenty years ago.

Motorbike engines started one at a time.

Mum yelled into the phone, "I better go, but thank you! You've made me feel a million bucks!"

Skye yelled down the phone over the noise of the engines, "I've told Chooky to take care of you. Only you would do this, Amy, you mad woman! Call me when you get back to Cairns!"

My mum was like some kind of C-Class celebrity—everywhere we went someone knew her. God knows how, because we'd lived in a little country town for most of our life and she had literally hibernated since Dad died.

There were a dozen men who rode forward from the concrete landing outside the shed to test out their brand-new machines. I zipped up my jacket, pulled on my helmet and gloves, and started my engine. I tapped for first gear, feeling the firm tension in my hand as I let the clutch out, and away I went. Everyone did a couple of figure-eight circuits of the lawn in front of the shed, then we pulled up in a line for Deb, Gus's wife, to take a photo. We were the first tour of the season.

Dirt and Dust

We all sat on our bikes facing the shed and Mum, who was still on the concrete landing. Everyone cut their engines while they waited. Mum was slower to get organised after the surprise phone call. She had her helmet and jacket on but was wrestling with her gloves. Finally, she looked ready, and all eyes were on her—she looked like she had never been on a motorbike before. And then, just to surprise us all, Mum accidentally hit the horn with a cheeky *Beep* instead of the ignition button. *Oh, for fuck's sake, Mum!* Was she playing the fool here? I couldn't believe it. My eyes nearly rolled back in my head, I wanted to disown her. She threw both gloved hands up in the air in a gesture of 'I'm just kidding' while her helmet nodded backwards and forwards with laughter. But I wasn't really sure if she was joking, and no one else knew her well enough to know if this was her humour, or if she was a complete and utter motorbike riding dud!

Mum over revved the engine and bunny hopped forward before joining the line-up on the end and not next to me, thank goodness. *Can this get any worse? This is like bad humour 101. Or like a scene out of Mr Bean!* I was sure everyone was thinking, 'How the fuck is this woman going to ride over a thousand kilometres on that bike?'

Deb snapped our tour group photo, then we started our engines again. My adrenaline was pumping from the anticipation and excitement. We took off down the driveway in a line after Gus. Sand and dust flying. Me, midfield, and Mum, somewhere at the back.

Onto the bitumen we went and carved our way up the Macalister Range. We pulled into a roadside stop which was a magnificent lookout, high above the tropical rainforest. I could hear Mum travelling up the mountain—the last rider—revving the crap out of her DRZ400. She came flying around the corner, missed a gear change and I thought, 'I hope she sees us and stops.' Just as she pulled in, we were all ready to go again. *Oh, man, I hope we are not waiting for her the whole time!* I could sense everyone else was thinking the same thing. *The only lady rider, my mum, can I just quietly die somewhere else right now?*

She whipped her helmet off and was smiling from ear to ear as if she had just won the Dakar Rally. *Bloody hell, we've still got such a long way to go.* Mum took a selfie with all of the motorbikes lined up behind her and I tried not to visibly shake my head as I groaned and hoped she didn't behave like a tourist at every photo opportunity. I could hear my own eighteen-year-old boy voice complaining in my head; *Muuuuuuuuum! This is serious motorbike riding stuff!*

Amy. First stop, Macalister Range.

At lunch on the first day, we stopped at the Mount Molloy pub and ordered steak sandwiches. By the time Mum putted into town and found the ladies toilets, she didn't even have time to eat. I started to make small talk with some of the other fellas while Gus spoke to Mum, "I'm going to have to charge you double for this trip, Amy."

Concerned, after she had just signed two waiver disclaimers to pay for the damage on both of our bikes, Mum replied, "Oh, why's that?"

Gus joked with her, "You haven't stopped smiling yet."

Flashing her big white teeth in reply as she spoke, "I can't believe I'm actually doing this."

Gus nodded in the direction of her lunch, "Did you want to take your sandwich with you? You haven't eaten it."

"I can't eat it, I'm too excited!" she replied, beaming.

After lunch we split into two groups—Gus wanted to test our riding ability so he could gauge how hard to push us on the ride. Mum went one way, and I went the other. By the time we met up that night at Cape Tribulation, I noticed Mum had dried mud caked up the side of her. Not just her boots, but her pants, jacket, everything. She was still smiling, though, so everything must have been okay.

I was smart enough not to mention the mud, but just then, Doug, the guy that asked Mum if she was riding earlier this morning, rocks up and says, "Hey Amy, did you come off?"

Mum replied, still smiling, "Might have!" Smiling was her cover for everything. Nervous, scared, sad, or happy, you'll always get a smile. It will just be the width that varies.

"Was that before or after lunch?" Doug enquired.

"After, why?"

"That's okay. My son, Shane, fell off *before* lunch!"

And all three of us laughed. Maybe my mum wasn't as hopeless as I thought.

Cape Tribulation was intense. Thick green foliage grew right up to the side of the roads. We pulled in for the night at a caravan park and were assigned cabins. It was good to peel off our sweat soaked riding gear and hit the showers. Our tour group met up at the bar for a drink and to order dinner. The tables on the deck had a sheet of paper that said 'RESERVED for Gus's dirt bike crew' written in a rough combination of capital and lower-case letters. I wouldn't normally notice that stuff, but when your mum was a schoolteacher, you usually saw things differently. Mum didn't say anything about the writing, but she smiled and raised her eyebrows. That was the thing about my mum, she wasn't your stereotypical schoolteacher. She wasn't bossy or a stickler for the rules; it was almost like she enjoyed breaking them.

She was a forty-year-old rebel of the kindest-kind. Those rough kids at school? Well, the naughtier they were, the more she liked them. She didn't do the power struggle thing; instead, she befriended those kids and explained their own behaviour back to them. It was almost like they thanked her for kicking their arses. It was bizarre, but it worked.

We went to the bar and Mum bought two schooners of beer. The barman asked to see my ID and as Mum was paying for the drinks, she joked with the barman, "Hey, how come you didn't ask me for ID?"

He leaned on the bar and replied, "Sorry, young lady, can I please see your ID?"

Mum smiled, and the crow's feet that she called 'smile lines' wrinkled up at the corners of her eyes. We stood at the bar, clinked our glasses together and said cheers before we sucked the froth off the top, then made our way back to the rest of our tour group.

In a crazy, little dark bar memory-flash moment, I thought about the day we said goodbye to Dad…

It was a rough day. The three of us; me, Mum and Jacinta, stood there next to a casket that contained my dad. Afterwards, Mum took us to an Irish bar. The place was empty on a Friday at lunchtime, and we tried to eat something but couldn't. It was weird how grief left us with zero appetite, even when the food was sitting there right in front of us. Mum bought me a beer. "For Dad," she said. At fifteen I felt guilty, but I gulped it down anyway.

It was funny how memories popped into your head like that; having a beer in a pub on the day you say goodbye to your dad. *Keep moving, boy, don't get stuck!* I told myself as I followed Mum's stumpy ponytail out on to the deck.

Tonight, we were staying at PK's Jungle Village at Cape Tribulation. It was time to mingle and suss out who belonged to who regarding the other riders on our tour. We'd already met big, barrel-chested Doug and his son Shane who won the prize for being the first to fall off his bike, *before* lunch!

I'd always been observant, and thought I was pretty good at picking people and personalities, but I got one person wrong. There were three guys all roughly about the same age, late-twenties, standing in a group. I thought they were three brothers, but it turned out there were two brothers, Chance and Chase, on tour with their parents Dave and Marg, and one fella on his own. The odd one out was smaller and wirier than the other two. His name was Jethro Rathburg. I had an internal giggle to myself when I shook his hand, feeling grateful on his behalf that with a name like Jethro Rathburg, he didn't speak with a lisp. Everyone called him Rat.

We had another beer and enormous chicken parmigianas each for dinner before hitting the hay. Mum and I were sharing a cabin. She curled up in her little single bed like a kid, but I'm six-foot-three, so my feet hung over the end and my head was right up against the wall. It wasn't long after we closed the door that whoever was in the cabin next to us was snoring like a diesel generator. All I could think was, *I hope that doesn't happen every night.*

CHAPTER 2

WHY?

Day two dawned and we saddled up for…well…we didn't even know yet.

Gus and the tour guides had already checked over our bikes and had them ready to roll by the time we finished breakfast. We started our engines and travelled a few short kilometres down the road where we met our first water crossing for the day—the water was so clear you could see the smooth, worn rocks at the bottom. With some breakfast in my belly and the first day nerves gone, I felt more confident. Everyone, including myself, made it through the water and waited on the sand bank on the other side…everyone except for Mum. Everyone was watching her.

As Mum entered the water on her bike, she hit a rock and threw her head back and laughed, before hitting another rock and laughing again. She started tank-slapping as the handlebars flicked out of control and hit a third underwater rock. Then down she went with a *splash*. Mum drowned the motorbike. Men came running from everywhere, not to save Mum, but to get the motorbike out of the water! She was absolutely soaked. I watched as Mum stood up and said, "Did anyone get that on video?"

In absolute synchronicity, three men with go-pros on their helmets replied, "Yep!" I wanted to back away into the rainforest scrub and disown her. *Jeezus, Mum!*

After a quick pit-stop on the side of the track to drop the water out of the intake, we were off again. Through the rainforest, we rode over slippery, black silt tracks of the Daintree and then some of the roughest, steepest terrain I'd ever seen. Honestly, I was motoring up these washouts over loose gravel, wondering how the hell I would stay on. I couldn't see the top, and I sure as hell wasn't game to look back at the bottom. It took an enormous amount of strength, skill, and concentration. Then doubt about my own ability started to creep in. *Am I able to hack a week of this?*

Experimenting with different strategies across the terrain, I tried to ride on the hard, high sided camber of the track. After only about a hundred metres, I dropped the bike, dumping it fair and proper. With legs so long, though, I literally laid the bike down and stepped off. My heart and mind were racing, adrenaline pumped thick and fast through my veins. I quickly stood up and got the bike upright, hoping that no one was coming up the steep incline behind me as they would have to dodge my bike. The track was too narrow, and any closer to the edge would have been an irretrievable drop off for the bike and me.

After hauling the bike upright, I started the engine and straddled the bike with the tyre in the middle of the washout rut, and then motored like hell until I got to the top. I took a deep breath and muttered to myself, "Whose fucking idea was this?" It was only day two and we still had a thousand kilometres to go! I followed my own front tyre to where the hill started to flatten out and eventually, with a breath of relief, I saw the other yellow tour bikes among the tall grass and trees on the ridge.

Parking my bike, I pulled my helmet off and sat there to appreciate the view. The Bloomfield River stretched below us in a spectacular serpent-like curve. I took in a few breaths of appreciation. A quick flick of a smile from Gus told me I was doing okay—it was nice to have that unspoken approval from someone else, and it was a real thrill to have made it this far. I took a big slug of water out of my CamelBak and waited.

*The Bloomfield River stretched below us in
a spectacular serpent-like curve.*

It took a while, but I was relieved when I could finally hear Mum coming up the track. She parked her bike on the ridge to overlook the river just like everyone else, but as she pulled up, her helmet was bobbing because she was laughing her head off and talking flat out!

"Oh my god, Riley! I nearly lost my bike off a cliff! I dropped it twice in one spot. I just couldn't get going again!" When Mum had a drink and settled, she admitted her confidence took a massive dive, just like mine. It was almost the same story. She told me she nearly cried because it was so steep and couldn't pick up her bike, and Ralph, one of the tour guides, followed along behind to make sure she made it. He even gave her a double dink for about twenty metres up the hill to where there was a slightly flatter spot before she jumped back on the bike and got going again. And just like me, she made it!

By this stage I realised Gus was a man of very few words. I had to watch him carefully to know when it was time to ride because there were no grand announcements. It was simply that Gus would finish his cigarette, put his helmet on and ride away. And by that stage, everyone was pulling on their gloves and helmets in hot pursuit of which ever direction he disappeared in.

Mum had snuck off down the hill behind a tree for what she called 'a picnic wee', and when the sound of motorbikes kicked back into life, she was busy racing back up the hill still doing her pants up. I felt that internal pull of not wanting to be left behind by the men yet needing to wait for Mum. I couldn't tell her to hurry up because she had only just got here, so I waited, all geared up and ready to ride. Mum was half joking, half serious and said, "I wish he would give me five minutes notice, or a head start! I'm a girl you know. I don't just hop on and ride away like you boys." I knew what she meant, but I still impatiently wanted to go.

Down towards the river we rode. A cyclone had been through only a month before, so the crossing was gushing with water. My eyes were popping out of my head. *Is this where we are going to carry the bikes? That's a hell of a lot of water!* I'm sure Gus was secretly watching us all hiding our anxieties with our individual, uncomfortable, nervous twitches. I thought and felt like he was deliberately not saying anything, letting us all sweat. And then he smiled, turned around and rode back up to the lookout. *Phew!*

We regrouped at the top of the hill. Already, the sensation of dread was starting to overwhelm me. We had to ride *down* the track where I dropped my bike once and Mum dropped hers twice. I thought it was too late to worry about it now, though.

I'm not sure if you could call it 'riding' but going down that track I had to literally pad my foot breaks on and off, feather my front brake, and hold the bike steady and upright between my legs. It was a combination of balance between throttle, clutch, and brake to skid and slide my way down the same washouts for at least a hundred metres. I finally got to a point where I could actually ride the bike forward instead of sliding sideways. I straightened my handlebars up when I could see the bottom of the hill, slapped myself twice on the chest and yelled towards the sky, "My dad would be so fucking proud of me!" and motored all the way to the bottom. I accelerated straight onto the bitumen and travelled at speed again with the thrill of achievement in my soul and a smile a mile wide.

For morning teatime, Chooky and Marg had a table set up next to the truck and we waited near a waterfall for Mum to catch up. She wanted a picture with this beautiful backdrop. I put my arm around her, thinking that day two was epic so far!

Day two was epic so far!

After morning tea ended, we rode on the bitumen for a few hours and pulled up at a place called the Lion's Den for dinner and to stay the night. The weather was warm, so our travelling party headed to the creek for a few beers and a swim.

We did some washing and then headed back to the pub. After dinner, Gus moved over to our table. He congratulated Mum and I on our first two days of riding and ensured us that the road both flattened out and was a bit easier over the next couple of days. Following that, we would hit the sand in the north. After some small talk, Gus looked at both of us and asked, "Amy, Riley, what on earth is a mother and her eighteen-year-old son doing on a trip like this?"

Mum and I looked at each other knowing this question was coming. People were always curious. I got it. I understood.

Mum replied, "Well, we had planned to do this trip when Riley finished high school. I thought my husband and Riley would ride, and my daughter, Jacinta, and I would be the pick-up crew behind them. But…it didn't quite turn out like that…"

Gus nodded, but maintained gentle eye contact with Mum.

Mum took a little breath and continued, "My husband took his own life nearly three years ago. He loved to ride, and when he was struggling this is what we would talk about. This trip. Ride to The Cape. You know, kind of like a big carrot. I'd be busy convincing him there were good things to look forward to…"

Sucking on his cigarette, Gus thoughtfully said, "I see…"

In some ways it was a relief. Now Gus knew what our motivation was, our reason for being here.

Gus took up the slack in the conversation now that our secret had been spoken aloud. Making motions with his stumpy fingers that looked like they needed some WD40 to lubricate the joints, Gus explained we were about to criss-cross the east and west coast of the peninsula, all the way to the tip of the country. I wasn't sure whether I felt pathetic or brave for thinking Mum or I could do this. This trip wasn't exactly 'pay your money and have a cheap thrill', it wasn't for people who had sat on a bike once or twice. Yet here we were, green as all hell and doing it.

I told Gus about my dad who was six-feet-four and rode a red a KLR650–a bike Dad made look small. I told him how Dad used to snorkel at the beach around all of the bombie-corral with me and my little sister. Dad was a chef by trade, he played cricket and was a water skier before us kids came along. Dad had a windsurfer when he was a teenager. I told Gus when Jacinta and I were young we lived on a dairy farm in north eastern Victoria. Mum always maintained that Dad was the best version of himself when they were farming. He was observant and methodical. Everything had its place and Dad worked hard. Mum said her measure of tough was when they had us two little kids, three-hundred cows to calve, and Dad being suicidal. There were a few transitions in the family which included my grandfather passing away. Drought hit hard and there was family turmoil between my dad and his siblings. It was never very comfortable between the three of them. Dad always felt like the black sheep, like he was the little brother that could never be good enough, no matter what he did. Mum didn't want to leave the farm, but they packed everything up in a fortnight and left. She explained to us kids that Dad needed a fresh start.

Mum smiled in acknowledgement as she listened to me re-tell all the stories about Dad to Gus. She had this way of covering her teeth with a small smile when it hurt deep in her heart. Mum leaned over and gave me a brief hug and a kiss on the temple, then said goodnight before excusing herself.

There was a bit of a pause after Gus and I watched Mum disappear into the darkness. Doug moved over to our table with his drink—I didn't know whether he heard the first part of the conversation or whether he guessed what was going on. Gus bought me a beer from the bar, and it was the first time an adult man who was old enough to be my dad, shouted me a beer. I felt like a boy-man—not really a boy anymore, but not yet a man, either.

Gus waited until Mum was out of earshot, and nodded in her direction, asking, "Is your mum okay?"

"Yeah…" I felt like an adult again—Gus genuinely asked, and he valued my opinion, and it felt good. "Sometimes she's really sad. She doesn't always cry, but sometimes she's just quiet." I paused. "She calls it 'the stone wall of grief.' Her face doesn't really scrunch up anymore, she's past that bit, but tears just run. They leak out when she's driving the car, grocery shopping, or sometimes eating dinner. I don't know, just stuff like that. Odd times."

Sipping from his schooner, Gus asked me, "Are *you* okay?"

I shrugged, but I thought about that feeling of grief like I'm the wombat-eating carpet snake with a dislocated jaw and a bad case of indigestion.

Gus enquired, "How old were you when your dad died?"

We sat side by side, looking at the empty space across from us where Mum had been sitting. I replied, "Fifteen. My sister, Jacinta, was thirteen."

Gus was quiet and careful. He asked, "So you knew what was going on?"

"Yeah."

Gus continued, "I hope you don't mind me asking, but how did you find out? You know…that your dad was…gone?"

I took a sip of the frothy head off the beer. "The local cop came to school to tell Mum. We live in a little country town. Mum's a high school teacher. Everyone knows everything about everyone. Paddy wasn't just the local cop; he became like family to us."

Doug and Gus both nodded in understanding.

I continued, "Dad always went to work. He never had a day off. So, when he didn't turn up to work on a Monday morning, Mum knew straight away…"

I paused. Gus didn't say anything. He waited. I realised this was the first time I had to answer questions about Dad without Mum.

Gus nodded thoughtfully. "Do you mind if I ask, why? Do you know…"

"If we knew why, we wouldn't be sitting here. He wouldn't be dead. Someone would have done something…"

Doug graciously asked, "What do you think about it?"

"What? Suicide? I think it's a dirty word. It's dirty for whoever finds them. It's dirty for whoever has to clean up. It's dirty for the families. It's not shameful like it used to be, but it is still dirty. And it's confusing. I sometimes think Dad was selfish for leaving us, especially when I see Mum do something that Dad should have done—"

I wasn't usually outspoken, so it caught me by surprise that I said what had been bubbling just below the surface of my teenage skin. The two men didn't interrupt, they let me keep talking.

"—Like we had this random guy turn up at our house one night, full of drugs. He was under our house, then he'd disappear for a few minutes, then next minute he was banging on the wall outside my sister's bedroom. Then he'd disappear again. You should have seen Mum; she went into kill mode! She was more dangerous than the guy on drugs."

Doug and Gus both smirked at the thought of my little mum turning into Bruce-fucking-Lee and knocking this unknown stranger into another dimension!

"But it was so unfair—she was jumping out of her skin for weeks afterwards. No one thinks about that stuff. Fine, Dad, whatever, take yourself out, but who the fuck looks after your family when you're not there? Someone else might out of pity or sense of duty, but it's your family. Man, that's your job as a dad and a husband…"

The two men nodded in agreeance. I kept talking, unsure if I was all warmed up because of the second beer, but with the two men still listening, I didn't feel like I was telling tall stories. It was easier to talk to strangers about Mum and Dad. No pity. No victim status. No prior knowledge or bias. They were just words about two people they didn't know.

"Dad was like a gentle giant most of the time, but then he could blow up really quickly. No real words or arguments, he'd be volatile, and we never really knew why. Sometimes if Dad had been at home without us, Mum would tell us to wait in the car while she went into the house or shed first. I didn't realise until we got older that Mum was checking to make sure it was safe—so me or my sister wouldn't find him. Mum knew, she knew for a really long time."

Doug nodded in acknowledgment while Gus shook his head and said, "That's so unfair that you lived like that, waiting."

I swallowed that stupid lump in my throat that I got when emotions ran high. I thought about Mum with her cool exterior but constantly in fight or flight mode for her entire married life. My brain tracked back to Dad, and I spoke my thoughts to the two men sitting in front of me, "And then I feel awful. I question if there was something Dad couldn't tell us; some trauma, some shit that happened that he couldn't cope with? I bloody well feel sorry for him. Whatever was going on must have been pretty fucking bad in his head and in his heart that he had to escape from it permanently…"

The people on the next table over from us were laughing loudly which snapped me out of the intensity of the conversation at our table. The three of us swallowed more beer in a half time pause.

Doug was trying to bring a lighter edge to the conversation, he asked, "At the time that he died, do you think your dad still loved your mum?"

"Yeah, but it's like he just wanted her all to himself. He loved us kids, too, but he wanted all of Mum's attention, and it was like he would supress being jealous or something. I can't quite describe it."

Doug spoke again, "The reason why I ask that is because my wife is a doula. Do you know what a doula is?"

I shook my head in a motion of *no* and sipped my beer. It was my turn to listen.

"A doula is like a midwife so people can have their babies at home. Sort of like a birth coach."

I nodded a *yes* in time with Gus and listened as Doug spoke in his big, gentle man voice. I didn't expect him to be talking about love and babies. "Steph always talks about how the most underdeveloped area of her work is helping new dads understand what their role is." Doug moved his big meaty fingers into the shape of a triangle and kept talking, so proud of his wife's profession.

"She describes this triangulation of the relationship between the mum, dad, and baby. Everyone is learning their new position in a family, but the dad just feels ignored or not important anymore because the baby gets the love and attention that he used to get. It's like men need someone to explain the psychological shift that is about to happen to prepare them before the baby arrives. They know their role is to provide and protect, but they need to know how to love their partner when she is sensitive in her body after birth and be aware of her emotions—to be patient. It's a tough time for everyone."

There was a respectful pause, and I had to let that sink in. I hadn't thought about any of that. I had been the baby in the triangle of love, not the dad.

Doug spoke slow and steady, "A respectful man can do that naturally; a man that appreciates a woman's body and the physical and chemical, emotional process and change of having that baby. But the wife needs to know how to make her man feel important, loved and included. Some men do that themselves by inviting themselves in all the time—by helping because they want an active role in their kid's upbringing. But some withdraw and resent the baby and their partner for not loving them the same as before the baby arrived. It depends on the partnership and the personalities. It can be perfectly okay, or it can be really difficult."

While we listened to Doug, Gus sucked on another cigarette and I played with a beer coaster that had a picture of a lion on it. Maybe this was the law of the jungle talk that no one ever gave my dad.

"Men need to know they are responsible for bringing that baby into the world. That they have just created a family and share that type of love, and not just one-on-one love with their partner. Families don't have the structure and sharing like they used to, people put a lot of pressure on themselves when it's just a couple nowadays."

Gus looked at Doug like he had never heard those words before but understood every single thing he said. Daddy-Doug continued on a more social tone rather than a teaching tone, "And in the blink of an eye, you little babies are all grown up! I love having teenage kids, young adults to do stuff like this adventure ride. My wife would never have ridden to Cape-bloody-York on a motorbike, and I wouldn't expect her to. But I can have a great time motorbike riding with my son. Having a family is fabulous, it's the best thing in the world." There was a thoughtful pause as if Doug wasn't sure whether to say the next thing on his mind or not. "I feel bad for you, Riley, that your dad skipped that part, mate, but by crikey you're lucky to have a mum that wouldn't miss it."

I smiled and nodded, looking into my beer, the tide was halfway down the glass. "I think all of the reasons why Dad fell in love with Mum eventually drove him crazy. My mum *is* crazy!" I smiled. "Not psycho-erratic kind of crazy, just spontaneously crazy. You never know what she's going to do or say. She has this spirit. It's like you can't hurt her. She does stuff like load us into the car to chase sunsets. Or take us for walks in the dark to soak up the stars. She makes me and my sister do stuff, like turn the stereo up full blast, and wear sombreros while we help her paint the front fence of our house on school holidays. I don't know…stuff like that. The whole neighbourhood thinks we are nuts, but at the same time, somehow, I think they want what we've got. It's like you can't say no to my mum, she never asks us to do anything, she just gets started and we end up helping. She's kind of, *irresistible*, like that."

Smiling at the memory of the three of us painting the front fence, I added, "They never used to fight much, Mum and Dad, that is, but sometimes you could feel the tension. Especially when Dad would come home from working away. It was like he didn't know how to be with us as a family again. It was uncomfortable for everyone. When Dad was anxious or depressed, Mum would take him a cup of coffee, or a cold beer when he was working in the shed. It was like she used to make excuses to go and check on him. Make friends, try again… re-connect…"

Gus stood up and said, "I gotta go syphon the python!" before disappearing into the dark to take a leak. Doug and I took that as a cue for conversational break and joined the line up next to a giant fig tree.

CHAPTER 3

Week-Long Therapy Group for Men!

We resumed our seated positions on the outside deck of the Lion's Den bar. Doug, being a lot more conversational, a lot more of a talker than Gus, asked, "So what happened mate? Because there's no real reason other than the fact that your dad was clearly struggling."

I replied, "Dad loved Mum but, in the end, I think his own insecurities ate him alive. One day they argued about money, he cracked it and smashed up the house. He'd been controlling everything for months to the point where Mum had no access to money. And it was not like she wasted it; it just costs money to live! *Dad* cut up the bank cards. *Dad* bought the groceries. *Dad* only gave Mum cash when she asked for it to pay for our swimming lessons or if there was something on at school—"

In defence of Mum, Gus butted in, "—But your mum is a teacher, didn't she have her own bank account?"

"Nah, everything went into *their* account, it had always been like that. She trusted him. Mum had always managed the money, and just thought that when Dad got all controlling and cut up the bank cards it was like a game to him. She honestly thought he'd just give up after a while when he realised there was no extra money to be saved."

Gus was looking at me through a side glance and asked, "Riley, you do know that's wrong, don't you? You can't control someone in a relationship like that. It's actually domestic abuse."

I responded, "I didn't know what it was, but I knew it was unfair."

I felt awful. I had just shared my mum and dad's personal relationship struggles with two strangers.

Doug snorted with a thoughtful scoff of air through his broad nostrils. "My wife has her own money, I have mine, and then we have ours. That's how come Shane and I are doing this trip, I saved up for it and the girls are going to Bali later this year. When the kids were little, I was earning and Steph was home with the kids, so yeah, everything was ours, but we discussed the financial decisions so we both knew what was going on. There was limited cash, but we had a family and one income. When Steph went back to work, we agreed to have *yours*, *mine* and *our* bank accounts which were for expenses, but it's never 50-50, that's not fair either, I earn more money than she does."

Gus was sucking on another cigarette and puffed out, "Deb runs our business while I'm away doing tours. I don't care what she spends the money on as long as there is enough for beer and cigarettes, and a bottle of scotch at Christmas." He laughed wholeheartedly, then added, "I know I'm providing for my family by loving what I do. I trust Deb to do whatever she needs to do. The proof is there, we've got a nice home, we can help our grown-up kids, what more can a man want?"

Doug nodded. "The point is, Riley, you need to know that there is more than one way to skin a cat. Controlling a person through friendships or money is never going to end well, in fact it is coercive control and it's very short-sighted. And whether your dad deliberately did that or whether he started controlling things because he wasn't in control of himself is the point that screams alarm bells. As a young man, I want you to know it doesn't have to be like that…it *shouldn't* be like that. A relationship is only going to work when you respect and trust each other. And if it's not like that, you need to walk away."

Gus did the sidewards glance thing at me again. "Did your mum stand up to him?"

"Yeah, she subtly did. But after months of the money controlling thing, Dad was getting worse. He broke his hand when he punched the wall in the loungeroom. The first smash was so loud I thought he shot himself. Mum ran from the kitchen to the loungeroom. He was in a fit of rage and there were four holes at head height where Mum and I had been standing on the other side of the wall. Those punches were meant for us…

"Don't get me wrong, Dad was a good guy, but when he got filthy angry, it was like his words couldn't come out and he would lose it. After he broke his hand, Mum told him he had to leave—this wasn't the first time he had smashed stuff—she told him, point blank, he needed professional help because he wasn't listening or respecting her anymore."

Both of the men nodded a slow, sad nod of understanding.

"Dad tried to bandage his own hand up and wanted to take one of us kids in the car with him when he drove to the hospital. Mum just said, 'No bloody way! I'll drive you.' And it made me realise that Mum had only ever left us with Dad about half a dozen times in our whole life. And she sure as hell didn't trust him driving when he was angry.

"There were times when I was supposed to go with Dad, I dunno, to Bunnings or something, and I dreaded it. I pulled back because it was like he would just give me a hard time for no reason. A couple of times when Dad was in a mood and I didn't want to go, Mum ended up telling me to get out of the car. She knew the situation could end badly. And it is bullshit when you want to stand up to your dad, but you're still a kid and you don't even know why he's shitty at you."

Doug spoke, "Your mum was keeping you and your sister safe, mate. That's why she had to tell him to leave. If he was reasonable, he would have understood that. People cannot behave that badly and think they can keep having one more chance. Actions speak louder than words, mate. She was right, there was nothing left for her to do, he had to help himself."

Slowly puffing on his smoke, Gus left a pause in the conversation and then added, "There's a fine line between loving someone and being loyal when you believe they will get better. And then there's wondering whether they are just having a tantrum to get their own way. It's hard when you love and believe that someone loves you back, I get it. It's just that, you have to be hurt an awful lot to start standing up for yourself. Especially when you never believe that stuff could happen to you."

I didn't expect grown men to talk like this, I hadn't been in the company of adult men who were so in tune with this genuine gentleness. I sure as hell didn't expect to experience that *here.*

My heart was heavy, but at the same time I could feel defensiveness bubbling inside me. This was where everything was so confusing deep in my core. I added, "I don't want to shit-can my dad. That's not fair; the man isn't here to defend himself."

"Yeah, I understand," replied Doug. "But you also need to talk about it, to deal with it, mate."

There was a little gap in the conversation and then Gus asked me, "Do you think your dad would have actually followed through and done this trip? Ridden to the Cape?"

I flicked the beer coaster between my fingers, then flung it onto the table like a card when you play poker. "Honestly, it would have come down to money. If he saw this huge amount of money being spent on *fun*, no, probably not. But that's the part Dad didn't understand…you have a life to make memories and create a story you are proud of. It's a balance between the two and I think being too financially 'locked in' depresses people. But then to contradict that, having no security scares people. Somehow you gotta hit it in between. Dad just didn't know how. Dad didn't know how to be happy or even satisfied."

It was Gus's turn again. He said, "Mate, I see them all the time, men that think the world is against them." His cigarette was jammed between two unbendable clutched fingers, he pointed his thumb towards his own heart region. "But the war is inside them. The world is a reflection of *who you are*. I don't want to sound all philosophical and horseshit, but it's true. Life is like a mirror. Some people get a raw deal either physically or financially or the family they were born into. But in a country like Australia, in a time like this, it's what you make it. It's your responsibility to make your own life as good as it can be. There's seriously no excuses to not live your best life."

Gus exhaled the smoke and kept going with his steady rhythm of talking, "And when men stuff up, they deal with it in one of two ways; they either pull their head in and try again, give their missus whatever they need and want to get on with life whether they are in it or not. Or they fight and bitch and carry on until everyone is exhausted and there's nothing left. That's why I don't understand what your dad did.

"He had a beautiful wife and family, and a job and a home, but he just couldn't realise what he had. The man had everything a man could ever want. He created it, and then ruined it. He should have been fighting to keep you guys together, not blow it up. It's not okay to do that!"

I got the feeling that Gus didn't normally get so fired-up about other people's business, so it took a moment to let the conversation find its equilibrium, its balance in silence again. Eventually, I looked from one man to the other and spoke, "Somehow, I think Dad was jealous that Mum was happy and settled with her job, her life. She never had grand plans. She loved her little school and living in a country town. It was like he couldn't keep us on the run anymore. Moving to a new house, moving jobs, moving towns. Mum just decided she loved her life, and he couldn't upset her anymore. She was relentless in the pursuit of getting on with living, no matter what, it was like she would laugh when things went to shit. Like everything was a dare to do better, go harder, give it one more shot…."

Gus chuckled and inserted, "I noticed, at the water crossing this morning!"

Week-Long Therapy Group for Men!

Jeez, was that only this morning? My god we'd fit a lot into this day!

Doug was still smiling about Mum dumping the bike in the creek and then he added, "Mate, your dad, he should have been so proud of your mum and you kids, not jealous. Sometimes people need to stop looking over the fence. Stop caring what other people are doing and get on with their own stuff. The grass is never greener somewhere else, and if it is, it's fertilized with bull-shit!"

Gus patted me on the back and swallowed the last of his beer. "That's enough coaching from two old motorbike riders for one night!" He looked at Doug and they both laughed. Gus continued, "Well, grasshopper, we'll talk again, but you've certainly had the weight of the world on your shoulders. I hope the next few days allows you to lose some emotional baggage and free up your future."

Waving my hand in the general direction towards the other motorbike men from our crew, I gestured 'good night'. My footsteps were heavy in my thongs as they crunched on the gravel back to the camping ground. Mum was on the top bunk, asleep, her breaths coming in and out at a gentle, steady, rhythmical pace. I crawled into my double sized bottom bunk, which still wasn't quite long enough. I tried to lay diagonally to get comfortable and eventually fell asleep. I was tired. Tired from two epic days of riding, but also tired before the lead up to this adventure. Tired from sharing our tragic story. Tired of trying to make sense of everything about Dad. Tired of subtly looking after Mum and looking out for my little sister.

I didn't know whether it was better to share it—share the circumstances, share the story. That was the ongoing dilemma; if you said something people thought you were a 'victim', but if you didn't say anything you weren't 'dealing with it'. The whole shitty circumstance was a tragedy, and as mixed up as it was, I still loved my dad.

I'm not sure how long I had been asleep, but I woke to the roar of laughter from men's voices outside. The Lion's Den Hotel must have closed, and they brought the party back to the campground. It was hard not to eavesdrop when the walls were so thin. Listening to their voices in the dark, I was able to figure out who was who, like piecing a jigsaw together.

Ratty must have two little kids and had split from his partner, and this motorbike ride was his freedom run, his 'I'm going to do something for myself' moment. I suspected Gus was there with all the other young blokes. Their voices would murmur for a while and then they would break back into a loud laugh. In the quiet serious talk, I heard Rat say something like, "Oh, for fuck's sakes, female orgasms are like a unicorn, they don't fucking exist!" I smirked to myself and imagined the other blokes out there smirking too. Who knew? There was no real verbal response from the other men, so Ratty kept talking, sharing his frustration with the outcome of his relationship. As I was dozing off to sleep again, I wondered whether this wasn't just a ride to the tip of the country, but if it was a weeklong drinking, fishing, and motorbike riding therapy group for men.

CHAPTER 4

Motorbike Meditation

Low clouds made visibility poor from the deck outside the Lion's Den Hotel where the riders sat for breakfast. I drank my apple juice and hoed into the baked beans on toast heaped with enormous rashers of bacon. While I chewed, I looked down the bitumen road in the direction where we would be riding. You couldn't see further than a hundred metres. I exhaled a short sharp breath through my nose. Dad used to do that. It was as if his mind was thinking but his lips weren't moving, and his mouth was saying nothing. It was like a judgement on an unknown thought. An evaluation, maybe? Mum called it the shitty sniff! But I just did it. *What was that?* Was it a feeling of disgust? Was the reverse-sniff an acknowledgement of something I didn't agree with, but it deserved no actual words of recognition? Because that would just be complaining about something I couldn't change.

Did I just disapprove of the low set clouds on the road blocking my view?

That was exactly how being left behind after suicide felt—surrounded in a cloud that you couldn't see out of. You couldn't see where you came from, and you couldn't see where you were going. You were just kind of…stuck there. And there was no point complaining because it was done, and there was not a thing any of us could have done about it. Especially now.

By the time we were ready to ride, warm misting rain had soaked everything in an intensity that can only be felt in the tropics. The sun had poked through the clouds and lit up the road as we motored onto the shiny bitumen, and then back into the thick dense clouds again. All in a cycle that kept repeating itself. I couldn't see anyone else. I had to stick to my side of the road, hold a steady speed, and trust I would come out the other side.

Hours on the bike was like motorbike mediation for men. Commonly referred to by riders as 'Helmet Time.' I'd ridden with mates my age, but it was always just fun; a laugh a minute. Teenagers like us were always doing something to create more action, more speed, more drama, more risk. We were playing—it was short bursts of racing around the paddock and then we'd find something else to do and drift away. But this ride was different. It required an element of endurance. Staying power. The determination to finish it. This wasn't like a cruise ship holiday where you paid your money, ate, drank, and danced your way to the destination! Fuck me! You had to earn it.

Long stretches of road gave me time to reflect on everything that had happened. I was safe to explore my memories in my own in helmet. My thoughts wandered to the day we found out Dad died…

I was the Year 10 school captain. When the afternoon bell rang at 3pm I had a crook feeling in my gut. Paddy's police car was parked outside the school and Mum was already sitting in her car, waiting in the carpark. *That wasn't normal.* I pretended not to notice and rode my pushbike home as per usual while Jacinta got a lift with Mum. It was only a few minutes between leaving school, cycling down our driveway and parking my bike under the house.

By the time I made it upstairs, I knew something was seriously wrong. Mum's face was still, and she did one of those small, tight lipped smiles. It was more of a grimace than a smile. She sat us down at the kitchen table and held our hands. "Paddy came up to the school today…he came to tell me…"

Mum told us that Dad had taken his own life.

There were no big gasps or a crying out in shock. The three of us knew; it wasn't exactly a surprise. It was like we had been waiting since November when Mum told him he couldn't live here anymore.

Mum's phone pinged with the arrival of a text message that broke our silence. She ignored it while the three of us hugged tightly together. I don't really remember what happened after that, but I do remember feeling heavy in my heart, and in my body.

Sometime in the middle of the night I heard Mum get out of bed. She was retching. An awful smell wafted into my bedroom from under the door. Her body was emptying its contents from every orifice. I wondered, *is that what happens when people get smashed with shock, grief, and sadness? Waves of anxiety hit you until your body literally aborts whatever toxic shit is inside?* I didn't know, I was only fifteen. I stared at the ceiling in the dark, feeling completely numb, and wondered why I wasn't crying. Eventually, I dozed off around dawn.

By the time morning came, Mum got up as per normal. She was drinking coffee in her dressing gown and spoke quietly to Jacinta and me while we were attempting to eat our breakfast. "You kids need to go to school today," she said. "I need to make a hundred phone calls to say the same thing, and you don't need to hear that. Right now, I think you need to be with your friends, and have a normal routine."

Jacinta and I nodded in between our mouthfuls of soggy cornflakes. We hadn't seen Dad for about eight months. After he punched the holes in the wall and broke his hand, we had only seen him once and spoke to him once on the phone. Then he cut the phone and the power off without warning, so that was it. We didn't even know where he lived. It wasn't like there was anything different today from yesterday. But it was weird to know that your dad was dead and not just living somewhere else. Not just working away, but not coming back at all. Ever.

After school we didn't exactly charge into the house like we normally did. I suppose we were waiting to see how Mum was after a whole day at home by herself. Jacinta was hunting around in the pantry, starving for something to eat. She paused to pick up a piece of paper from the bench that had a rough sketch drawn on it. "Mum, what's this?" She held up the piece of paper. Written in the middle of the page was 'Town of Dad'. It was a diagram in the shape of a cloud with dotted lines like roads running through it. There were different sections that said: Dad with Mum. Dad on holidays. Happy Dad. Angry Dad. Dad with me…

Mum took the piece of paper from Jacinta and gently put it on the dining table. We sat down in the same positions as yesterday, ate our snacks and listened.

"A psychologist came here to visit me today, to talk about what happened with your dad. She drew me this diagram and wanted me to share it with you. She called it the 'Town of Dad.' It has all of these

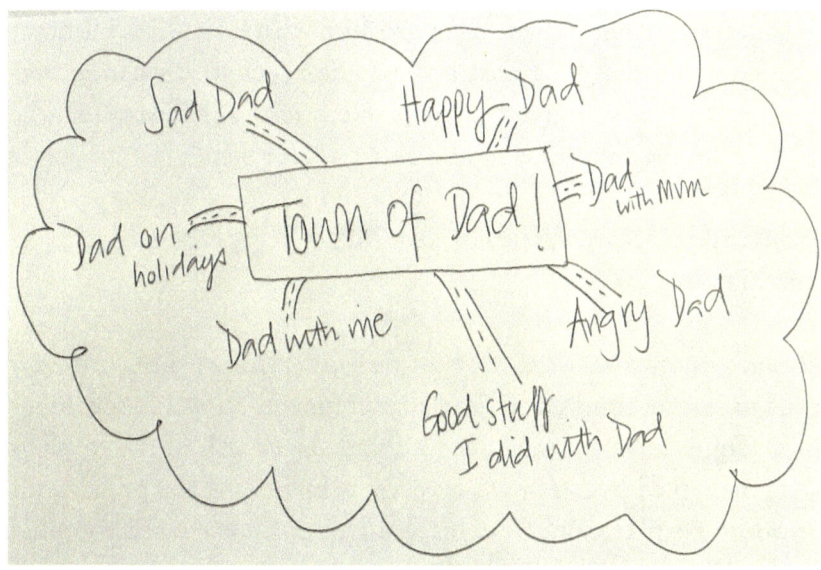

Town of Dad.

suburbs..." Mum pointed to Happy Dad and then moved her finger across the page before landing gently at Angry Dad.

Mum looked at us both. "When you are remembering or questioning everything, you are going to visit The Town of Dad. You are going to travel through the suburbs and then you'll turn around and go back through them again. And that's perfectly normal. But just don't break down and stay in the suburb of Angry Dad."

Jacinta and I munched and nodded. After a pause, typical curious thirteen-year-old Jacinta asked, "What else did she say?"

"We talked about how your dad could be moody and awkward sometimes. When he was anxious, it was like he was emotionally climbing a set of stairs. When his behaviour escalated that much, he didn't know how to get himself down. It was always me that would negotiate or change something or give him what he needed. He never learned to do that for himself. He couldn't identify when he was getting volatile or angry or anxious. He couldn't change tactics, he didn't have the strategies, and he didn't ask for help."

Jacinta asked, "Why was he like that, Mum? What happened to make him like that?"

"I don't know, pussy cat. Lots of reasons. His own insecurities, a need to control things, a sense of abandonment. He would say things like, 'You'll leave anyway.' I stayed and stayed. All of these things were magnified by stress, whether it was financial stress or just stuff at work or expectations from his family. But I knew when your dad was mad, he was just sad. He truly could have just apologised and tried again. I would have accepted anything. But he didn't. He hated me for trying to help him. He thought I was trying to change him. He took everything as an insult, as a personal attack. That's why I couldn't help him anymore. Your dad couldn't see how his behaviour was impacting on everyone else."

Jacinta and I both saw that for ourselves. Mum had talked about the same stuff in the three-hour drive from her mum's to Dad's mum's place on Boxing Day, six weeks after the holes in the wall incident. It was highly emotional for Mum, pouring her guts out in her mother in laws' loungeroom. She spoke about how Dad had been suicidal right from when she was pregnant with me. And now, all these years later, Dad wasn't communicating with Mum anymore. Someone other than her needed to know, so if Dad took his own life, it couldn't be a 'Mum only' secret anymore. Of course, our grandmother shook her head in disbelief. No one wanted to believe that their own forty-two-year-old adult son would potentially do that. How could he not love his own mother enough to live? Isn't it your job as an adult child to bury your parents? They took care of you, then you take care of them. *Isn't that what's supposed to happen?*

As I rode along, I was replaying the 'Town of Dad' conversation from that day in the kitchen, "I think the biggest issue for your dad is that he didn't have the words to help himself. He couldn't articulate his thoughts and feelings. He needed the simple words to use when he was struggling, stuff like…. 'I need help right now,' 'can you please help me?' But he didn't. Even when we separated, I just wanted him to be honest with me. I wanted him to say, 'I don't love you anymore,' or, 'I want to be by myself,' or 'I love someone else', whatever, just don't blow the show up and make it all someone else's fault. I just wanted him to be deadset straight and honest with me. This is *his* family!"

I finally said something in response to Mum, "Dad just couldn't talk like that though, Mum."

"I know, and his emotions would lock him up. And that's why I would try to help him, excuse things, cover for him, fill in the gaps, lay next to him at night and listen to him grind his teeth. I tried to prove that I loved him by staying physically close to him, not aggravate him, do whatever needed to be done so he didn't feel vulnerable. We never bailed on him."

Mum started to cry. It would have been a tough day. Jacinta gave her a hug and I got the box of tissues. We sat there and waited until Mum started talking again. "The pysch lady asked me if I knew what a narcissist was. I don't think your dad was deliberately narcissistic. When he was being unreasonable, I think he felt like he was losing control."

"Yeah, but how do you deal with a narcissist, Mum?"

"The only way to deal with anything, sweetheart, is to be honest. Honest with yourself, and absolutely straight-shooting honest with the other person. Say the words that need to be said without being overly emotional. The problem is, I knew your dad better than he knew himself. He hated that I could anticipate things. It's only a pattern of behaviour; once you've seen a pattern, you know what's coming next, it's predictable."

"What about depression, though? How do you even know when you are depressed?"

"I asked the psych lady about that, and she said if you are flat lining by not feeling your normal level of happiness, it's time to see someone. See your doctor, see your school counsellor, ring a helpline. I did those things *for* your dad, but he got blacklisted from the doctors for not turning up for appointments. He never followed through. God it was frustrating. I even offered to go with him if he couldn't talk about it. At least I could say what needed to be said. I could at least say what I was seeing to get the conversation started."

Jacinta kept probing, she asked with a thirteen-year-old level of urgency to understand why her Dad wasn't still existing earth-side, "Why though, why didn't he do it? Why didn't he get the help?"

Mum shrugged. "He didn't want people to think he was crazy. We argued about it one day, saying he didn't want to miss out on job opportunities if he was diagnosed with a mental illness. I said I didn't care about that because undiagnosed he could end up freakin' dead. And look what just happened.

"I'm filthy cranky. *He* didn't want a history of mental ill health, *he* didn't want to feel rejected or abandoned, but guess what he just gave you kids? Everything *he* didn't want *plus* a bloody death certificate and coroner's report to prove it! For fuck's sake! There's nothing

Motorbike Meditation

wrong with you kids, your dad just made a shit house decision by not dealing with it. But you two will get questioned for the rest of your life about your family's mental health history! Jeezus that's unfair!" When Mum gets emotional, her hands start telling the story. When she has finished spitting words of venom, she folds her arms in an effort to stop herself from spraying anymore…which was exactly what just happened.

As we motored closer to Cooktown, I could feel my eyebrows jammed together in a frown that made my head hurt. I had to snap out of the dead-dad conversation replaying in my helmet. The riders in front of me were slowing down. We collectively gathered to ride through town as a group. We hooked a right, then a sharp left and spiralled up toward the lighthouse. At the very top, one by one we cut our engines. Undoing my chin strap, I could hear Mum's motorbike engine roaring as she curled her way through the uphill left hand turns to catch up to us at the lookout. *Wrong gear, Mum,* I thought! She changed gears and started chugging on the next corner. She changed gears again and obviously thought it was better to roar than chug. The last rider always gets the most difficult place to park, and it was a shocker of an angle for someone with legs as short as hers. I smiled and ran over to make sure she didn't dump her bike in the gutter.

At the lookout we breathed in the stillness of the Coral Sea, where the water was the same colour as the sky. Our tour group paused for a photograph with the picturesque backdrop. Gus announced we could cruise around Cooktown for an hour or two as this was the last place, we would see any shops. "It's dirt tracks and roadhouses from here to the top of the country," he told us.

Chooky called out that he was doing a bottle shop run in the supplies truck and if we needed anything specific, now was the time to put in a request. Mum and I looked at each other, we spoke about this before we left home. Dad drank Jack Daniels on special occasions, so without a word between us, Mum handed Chooky a fifty dollar note and asked him to buy Dad's favourite so we could have a sip at the tip of Cape York.

Mum sent a Mother's Day gift to her mum in the mail, and then our time in Cooktown was up. Mum and I tailed the group of tour riders up the road. The excitement of being part of a motorbike gang as our engines rumbled was impressive. It gave me confidence, but I still felt a bit queasy in my guts. I had no idea what was coming next. It was almost like first day ride anxiety all over again. Gus's words were being juggled in my brain over and over: No shops. Endless kilometres of dirt roads. Sand. The Telegraph Track. The last frontier…

Us riders were stretched out over a couple of kilometres. I could see when the first person transitioned from bitumen to dirt. A plume of red dust led the way. One by one we crossed over. I held my throttle strong at one-hundred kilometres an hour and didn't even flinch. I was thinking about Mum behind me, hoping she did the same. Anything less than a steady hand on hundreds of kilometres of red dirt corrugations will have you bucked off in an instant.

I settled into the steady rhythm of rough, endless roads and stood up on my foot pegs to stretch my legs and skip across the top of the corrugations. I thought about how Dad was missing this, the natural highs. The butterflies in my guts had disappeared, and it truly felt like this was living. It wasn't easy, it was dirty, hard, and I had to think on my feet as I reached every obstacle, every water crossing, every pothole, every contrast from bitumen to bulldust. I had to ride it. What else was I going to do? Sook? Stay at home? Not try my guts out? Let my life go past me because I wasn't ballsy enough to just face it? It was true, people only became tougher, more resilient when they had to figure stuff out. If it's bad enough, you just make sure you don't mess it up a second time!

I wondered about Dad. He never gave anyone or anything a second chance…even himself. I was sure that's how he ended up dead. Why weren't *we* enough? Why wasn't *this* enough? Mum was trying to set up good things to look forward to, like this trip. Not just for *her*, for *him*, but *for us, as a family*. How come she knew how to look for the natural highs, but he didn't? She took us to climb mountains and swim in the sea. She saved the money to take us on our last family holiday to the snow. Stuff like that. We weren't rich, but we weren't poor either. We were very average. Maybe that was the problem for Dad; average wasn't good enough…I didn't know. Maybe just like gambling, Dad folded his cards early. Or was it fate? Did people just decide fate was a way of explaining an outcome they couldn't understand? Or was it acceptance that it was a choice not made by a person, but by some other power in the universe? I didn't know…I still don't know…

Dad wasn't much of a drinker. He would have a couple of beers at a time, and he probably only got drunk once or twice a year when we had visitors—and that was about the only time I ever saw him have a smoke, too. But I know in his past he smoked a lot of marijuana. Everyone says it's harmless, everyone thinks it's good for a laugh or helpful to relax. But I thought about whether people were depressed, so they have a *choof*, or whether being depressed is the after effect of it. Either way, it's an ongoing cycle.

When Mum and Dad separated, Mum was a nervous wreck, not sure if Dad was going to turn up at any time. After New Year, Mum was preparing to go back to work. She was in the local hairdressing salon when the hairdresser asked, "What the hell is going on, Amelia? Your hair is falling out, and you have this rash…"

Mum thought she was holding her emotion in and was going okay, but the anxiety of it all was ridiculous. Mum cried and told the hairdresser that she had to tell Dad to leave back in November.

The hairdresser responded with, "You need to go to the police straight away. I'm worried about you and your children…"

Mum used the 48-hour rule. She thought about it for forty-eight hours then went to the police station on Sunday morning. Paddy was sitting on the front steps of his house, right next door to the station, having a coffee in the sunshine. Mum said she felt like an idiot explaining the situation, saying it wasn't an emergency, but it had the potential to be. Paddy listened and asked her, "Why don't you have a DVO out on your husband?"

Mum paused, and replied, "I know I'm walking a really fine line here…but if the police turn up to give him a DVO, he'll either be that mad I'm not sure what he'll do, or he'll think that badly of himself, he'll kill himself."

Paddy nodded. "I see…"

Mum said her voice was shaking. It was the first time she'd verbalised those words out loud to anyone.

"I don't have any family here, and I can't tell anyone what's going on or it will just become town gossip. I don't want that. If I ring the station, I'll need you to come in a hurry. Please…"

Mum admitted she had this weird feeling Paddy would be the one to tell her something awful about Dad. It took eight months, but she was right.

The same week Mum spilled her guts to Paddy, she went to her doctor and got a referral. She had to fill out a survey to make sure she wasn't the one who was suicidal and to determine how urgent this situation was. It took six weeks before she could see someone. The counsellor,

Motorbike Meditation

Wayne, asked her about Dad's drug habits. Mum revealed that he smoked a hell of a lot of drugs between the age of seventeen and twenty-five, but nothing else that she was aware of. Wayne explained that the drug use basically stunted Dad's brain growth—meaning, the drug use stopped Dad's brain from developing skills like negotiation, problem solving, rational thinking and memory which led to his reduced satisfaction with life.

Through their discussions, Wayne pointed out that Mum was twenty and Dad was twenty-five, when they met. At that age and stage, it's all love, and in young adulthood you think you've found the person you want to share your life with. But by the time Mum was thirty and Dad was thirty-five, Dad still had a teenage functioning brain that included the 'everything is everyone else's fault' mentality in an adult body. Wayne also carefully suggested that because Mum is such a capable person, when Dad couldn't do something or if he was in a difficult place emotionally, Mum would put her superwoman cape on, and literally say, 'Don't worry about it, I'll do it. You have a rest. Just wait there and I'll take care of everything.' But that accidentally made Dad feel like she didn't need him. Unintentionally, it was empowering her and disempowering him. That was a massive realisation for Mum, and it was a hard pill for her to swallow. But it was the likely outcome and the honest truth.

The sun was starting to set as I followed the red, dust haze of riders into the Hann River Roadhouse. We kept our wheels rolling through the almost empty caravan park until we found Chooky and Marg who had the camp kitchen set up, out of sight.

It was too hot to stay fully dressed for a minute longer than we needed to, so everyone, including me, changed out of their riding gear. Ralph was on the listen; we could all hear Mum getting closer to the roadhouse. In typical mum-style, she could seriously ride a thousand kilometres but then get lost with two right-hand turns followed by a left in the freakin' caravan park! Ralph jumped on his bike with his singlet on and helmet off to lead her into where the rest of our crew were camped out of sight.

I had already cracked a beer from the big chest fridge in the tuck-truck and took a coldie straight over to Mum. She looked at me and brushed her nose, "Hey mate, you've got a bit of dirt on your nose!"

I mimicked her, brushed my nose and winked at her in return. "Hey Mum, you've got a bit of dirt on your nose!" She looked in her bike mirror, scrunched up her nose, laughed, and we clinked our stubbies together!

CHAPTER 5

Old Bull vs Young Bull

Chooky was cooking something that smelled like savoury beef mince on the open fire. I'd had two beers and my guts were growling with hunger. All of the riders had set up their little stretcher beds in the bush. They looked like randomly placed single, camouflage-green, coffins on legs—only the bare necessities were required from here to the top of the country. It was time for a well-deserved shower. I waited for Mum to grab her towel and we walked back towards the roadhouse. We chatted about the day's ride. A friendly emu that had been bobbing around the campsite decided to walk parallel with us along the tyre tracks. He was a funny character, eyeing us off and listening to our conversation.

"Mum, do you think I'm like Dad?" I asked.

"In what way?"

"I dunno…I was just thinking about it today," I replied.

"Well, you look like him."

"It's just that, I don't want to be as…I don't know…awkward."

"You're not, mate. You're a different character. A different personality to him. But there is the age old saying about nature versus nurture."

"What do you mean?" I asked.

"Well, it's like the contrasting sides of how you were born with a certain predisposition as opposed to the environment you were brought up in. So, I suppose it's like our family rules and expectations, experiences, that sort of stuff. Which is different to how your genetics determine some of our ways of being. Like addictive type personalities, that's genetic…"

"Yeah, right. So, you're saying I shouldn't smoke drugs?" I laughed, knowing Mum knew I was teasing her.

We walked for a bit further in silence listening to the click clack of our thongs. I could smell shampoo as I entered the roadhouse bathrooms. Bubbles were flowing freely from below the cubicle next to mine. An unseen man was whistling a tune, it was familiar, but I couldn't quite recognise what it was. I smiled. His personality filled the place with joy as the song bounced off the corrugated iron walls.

The man's shower turned off as I simultaneously turned mine on. He left not long after, and I really missed his presence. I finished in the gents and called out to Mum in the ladies, "Mum, I'm heading back now!"

"Okay, mate, I won't be long," she replied. Women always say that, 'I won't be long,' but they are. They take at least twice as long as men, at everything! I recognised another shitty sniff sneak out from my nostrils. Straight away I realised I had to change something here. I had to turn my thoughts around one-eighty-degrees, or I was going to be just like the cranky version of my dad. *Who cares how long it takes in the shower, she's allowed to take as long as she likes!*

Solo, I walked back towards the camp. After the escape of the second recognisable shitty sniff, I was thinking about how I didn't want Dad's suicide to be the biggest defining moment of my life.

It's so messed up when you meet new people, and they ask what your dad does for a living. And then they don't know how to hold a conversation with you when they realise he's dead. When this happens, I understand they are curious, but it's also shit-house when they ask, "So how did he die?"

Some people play this stupid predictable guessing game:

"Was he sick?"

"No."

"Was he in an accident?"

"No."

Then there is literally a deathly silence that only leaves one option. Suicide. And then when it dawns on them, there is a pause and they ask, "How did he do it?"

I honestly just wanted to say, "It's none of your business." If people cared about people, they wouldn't ask, and if I answered that question, it just becomes gossip. Another horrific detail for them to be gobsmacked about, and then they go ahead and tell someone else.

When people know how Dad died, but then ignore you or give you the cold shoulder because they don't know what to say, it's difficult. Life goes on as per normal for them, but we are left grieving, trying to find our new normal. Sometimes I just want to yell at them and say, "Hey, my dad died, I didn't. I still have to live, don't ignore me." They don't have to say anything, just stand there and show me they are with me.

When you stand next to someone who is in emotional pain, it means everything. There is nothing anyone can do. There are no words. No one can solve anything. It's done. People that pretend it doesn't matter have got it wrong. People that propose solutions or pretend to be happy don't know that I'm not emotionally ready for that yet. But close proximity of people when you are in emotional pain is everything. I think that's how Mum kept Dad alive. At times there were no words between them. She just stayed close to him. Reliably present.

Grandad used to use the term, 'the brake horse.' You know, the old steady horse that was in harness to go the same pace all day every day to teach the young horses not to flinch or shy or gallop off in a frenzy? Yeah, that's the brake horse. That's exactly what I needed to visualise when my own topsy-turvy combination of angry and sad thoughts started to race. *Just be the brake horse; blinkers on, go steady, same pace, same speed, same tempo, same direction.* Sometimes you need someone else to be the brake horse, or you gravitate towards people who are steady like that. But sometimes, I know I have to slow down and be my own brake horse when there is nothing and no one but me to rely on.

I stopped dead in my tracks, my thoughts interrupted. A skinny snake slithered across the track in front of me, bolting from left to right, and I watched as its tail disappeared into the grass. Standing there for a minute in the half-dark, I could see the familiar welcome flames of the campfire not too far away. I looked back toward the roadhouse shower block and decided to walk back and wait for Mum.

As I rounded the corner of the *Ladies,* Mum came out with her hair wrapped in a towel on her head—just like she used to do to me and my sister when we were little, and we'd dance around the loungeroom in our pyjamas. Mum was like her own cartoon character, and I smiled and scoffed a little laugh. She was both embarrassing and loveable all at the same time.

She smiled wide when she saw me, and spoke, "I thought you'd gone back to camp?"

"Yeah, decided to wait…it's getting dark…"

"Thanks, mate. That's what every gentleman would do."

I seriously didn't have to do much to make her proud. That was the privilege of being a kid who's loved, I supposed. Little did she know, though, I wasn't going to tell her about the snake. And maybe it wasn't safe for my little mum to be walking through an almost empty caravan park in the middle of nowhere by herself when the sun had already sunk below the horizon.

Mum spoke again, "D'you know what I learnt when we went on that trip to Europe?"

I shook my head *no* in the dark. Europe was another Mum and Dad bucket list item.

The three of us went; Mum, Jacinta, and me. It was a mad, busy, crazy, fast tour of the biggest-ticket items in the world. We spent the last few days of the whirlwind tour in Paris, the most romantic city in the world, without Dad. It rained the whole time. But the sun came out on the last night as we were going back to our motel after dinner. The three of us leapt off the bus and raced to the steps to look at the sun shining on the Eiffel Tower. Our Hungarian tour guide took the most magnificent photo of us.

I thought about that photo on our bookshelf at home—my arm around Mum while my sister kissed her on the cheek, and Mum smiling with her big teeth for the whole world to see happiness after so much sadness.

Riley, Amy, and Jacinta. The sun came out after three days of steady rain.

Paris was a long way from the contrasting Hann River Roadhouse. We kept walking and Mum kept talking...

"Do you remember the short, little Pakistani man that would hop off the bus first?"

I nodded, "Yeah, and he'd stand in the gutter and roll a cigarette."

"Yes, that's him," Mum said. "Well, it took me the first week of that trip to realise something."

"Realise what?"

"That I didn't have to be a tough, Aussie Sheila." (Mum used her best bogan voice when she said *Sheila*). "That man would hold his hand out to help everyone off the bus. I always thought, *I'll be right,* and waved him a 'thank you, but no thank you' gesture. And then about halfway through our tour, I decided I needed to just say 'thank you' and accept. I know I can do it myself, but if someone wants to help me, I just need to go with it. Appreciate it, accept it."

I nodded thoughtfully.

Mum kept talking, probably catching up on all the words she had no-one to tell when she was in her own helmet all day. "Do you want to know what I've been thinking about?"

Clearly, I didn't have to answer because she was going to say it anyway.

"I was thinking about how I can literally fall off that damn motorbike fourteen times in fourteen-hundred kilometres, and because I'm a girl, everyone slaps me on the back and helps me pick my bike up! They cheer for me when I'm last one into camp, like an hour after everyone else. But if *you* did that, as a young man, people would say, 'What's wrong with you, why can't you ride? You're hopeless!'"

Showing that I understood that comment, my head bobbed up and down in agreeance. It's true. That was exactly what happens.

"But do you know what else? I realised that toxic masculinity doesn't just happen in men. By the end of our marriage, I was mirroring toxic masculinity back to your dad."

"What do you mean by *toxic masculinity?*"

"Well, it's like when men don't show many emotions other than rage or bravado. They don't need anyone or anything, never snitch, suffer pain in silence, all that sort of stuff. Because your dad was like that, I did it back to him, so I wasn't perceived as *weak*."

"Hmm…I do it too, though, Mum."

"That's my whole point. If you've got a key person in your life that's like that, you become like that too. You can't help it, it's like a way of coping. But what have you noticed since your dad has been gone?"

I paused to think about it, then finally said, "That we've all been sad, but maybe we've all been allowed to be happier too?" I kind of felt guilty saying that—guilty that we loved and missed Dad but didn't feel under pressure or feel like he was going to sabotage happy moments by being cranky or just flat out negative.

While we walked and talked, Mum and I were nearly at the place where I saw the snake earlier. Mum was just saying, "Yeah, it's sad, I wish your dad could figure out—" when I interrupted…

Old Bull vs Young Bull

"—Hey mum, look at this…" and in the dusky, end of day-light, I pointed out the slither-mark across the sand in the track. Mum's eyes widened and her towel-turban on her head untwisted and half came undone.

Mum crouched down to look at the track, then looked up at me. Smiling, she said, "I used to be really scared of snakes." Mum stood back up and we walked in sync to the camp. "When you kids were little, I was petrified that a brown snake would bite you. Those bloody things were everywhere at the farm!"

I smiled, "Like the day you ferociously killed a snake in the garden? The one that was already dead?" We both heartily laughed as our own memories recalled Dad telling the story of Mum slaughtering a snake in between the rose bushes. Dad had already shot it in one clean shot and left it there, headless, until it stopped wriggling. A few hours later, Mum was gardening and got a fright from the moving snake in the bushes and started chopping it up like sushi with a shovel.

The memories—from a silly story that was so typical of our life, to Dad forgetting to mention he killed a snake in the garden, and then Mum making sure us kids weren't going to get bitten—made us warm with a familiar fondness.

Click-clack went our thongs in the red dust as we made our way back to the camp. Mum spoke, "After your dad died, I used to have this recurring dream that a giant carpet snake was laying at the foot of our bed, laying calmly up against the wall, resting…probably digesting something really big."

I looked at her profile in the half dark as we walked, and she talked. "I mentioned that dream to a really peace freak hippy friend. She told me not to be afraid because snakes symbolise transformation, regeneration, growth or the rebirth of something…"

Mum's words trailed off and in typical eighteen-year-old boy fashion, as we got closer to the camp, all I could think about was food, and dinner smelt so good. Mum and I hung our towels over the end of our stretchers and joined our crew around the fire.

There were two empty chairs next to Dave and Margy. Mum grabbed us a coke each out of the esky and chalked it up on the lid which doubled as the tally for the fridge bill. Dave spoke to me, "Not having a beer with dinner, young man?"

"Nah, I've already had two, that's enough."

"Good to see you know your limits. Nothing worse than being dehydrated halfway through a ride. Your mum tells me you're an apprentice mechanic; that's a great start in life, mate."

I could hear Mum and Margy chatting behind me. I was so glad it wasn't all men out here in the bush. I knew she'd be okay with it, but it was an unexpected bonus to have female company.

While I sat and talked about my apprenticeship, I could feel the scales on my own skin, they were itchy as if I was growing—still unsure if I was a boy or a man. Dave talked about all sorts of topics in his life. He was very proud to be riding with his adult sons on this trip. I felt a bit of a hole in my heart—guilty that it should be me with Dad right now. Confused, whether I was doing this trip for Mum, or if Mum was doing this trip for me, or whether it was really about us letting Dad go. Maybe it was all three.

Old Bull vs Young Bull

It was a nice, comfortable evening of conversation. After dinner, Mum said good night and headed for her bed in the bush. I wasn't far behind her. As I wrestled with the zippers on my fly screen that kept the mozzies out, I could hear that friendly emu still making throaty noises and bobbing around in the bush. I tried to get comfortable with my air pillow that took a whole three breaths to fill and thought about the conversation with Dave at the campfire.

Dave talked about how men needed to learn from other men. *It's true.* But when they get to forty-two years of age like my dad did, who's more alpha than them? Grandpa had passed away. So, who got to tell my dad he was royally mucking things up? Mum tried, but he didn't like it. Maybe that was why Dad changed jobs all the time and stayed away from his own family.

For God's sake, we'd moved thirteen times in my fifteen years of life. Dad was always restless, and I didn't know if that was his personality or whether he didn't want to address what needed to be addressed. So, we moved on. In his mind, in his life, he was always right. I got it. Everyone covers up their defects but how come some people identify what their holes are and work on them, while others are in denial? Maybe it was honesty. Honesty with yourself. Mum always wanted us to play sport or have a part-time job. She wanted us to stay 'coachable' and learn from other people in a type of self-discipline that had both internal and external rewards, and not guided by her. She said we had to learn from other people, not become too insular, especially after Dad died.

Dave said something I had never thought about; how men need to know when the time to transition from being a 'young bull' to an 'old bull' came. It was a sexist generalisation, but in his observation, on the whole, women did that transition much more easily and naturally in their family roles with children and then grandchildren. They care for others in each of their ages and stages in life. But men don't know what to do as soon as they aren't protecting or providing anymore. They lose their purpose. They think they've become redundant. And it hits their identity hard when they are no longer working. Who are they once their working life is complete? Maybe that was why Dad killed himself. Instead of trying to stay part of our family, he took Mum standing up to him as rejection rather than an opportunity to make changes to his behaviour, to recalibrate. And then when things at work got tough, he didn't feel good at that either. He just couldn't try anymore. He couldn't recreate a new purpose or reinvent himself. Or maybe he just didn't allow himself enough time to do that. People survive relationship break downs, they survive job losses. It doesn't mean they have to die.

Maybe I was naive. Maybe it was a privilege not to understand the weight of being saturated and eventually suffocated by depression, or the anger that comes with anxiety when you want it to stop. Dad was dangerous when he was angry. His emotionless blank stare that could turn into a wild eye was when you knew to get out of the way. Thinking about it now, three years later, Mum did an amazing job to manage him when he was irrational.

I wondered about how people survived life transitions. Like me right now, a school kid into a young adult. My friends were still the same, I still lived at home, I just went to work instead of school now. But what about later, like Dave said, from young bull to old bull? This trip was freakin' rough going. Dave admitted that he couldn't continue to ride hard anymore, so he dropped back in the pecking order after the first few days. Mum was always last in the line-up, so Dave found his place second from the back. Earlier in the night he was laughing with Mum about the rider's hierarchy, saying, "It's not too bad at the back, Amy, you're not choking on everyone else's dust all day!"

Dave admitted to finding the ride more enjoyable and a much better pace for his sixty-something-year-old body. Mum appreciated his guidance when he led her through another obstacle, water crossing, or waited at a junction where any of us could get lost by taking the wrong turn. There was no phone service, GPS, walkie-talkies or fancy communication systems out here. It was a matter of follow the dust from the rider in front or wait at a crossroad until the next rider can see you. Neither Mum nor Dave had anything to prove to anyone, only to themselves. To make it to the most northern point on the continent, Cape York, and just like me, they were doing it! Gus' words at the rider briefing echoed in my memory, 'This is a tour, not a race!'

So, what did Dave do when he realised, he had the expertise and experience, but not the endurance? He rode at his own pace and he reached back and helped Mum. Maybe that was it—the answer to this 'feeling redundant' conundrum. Maybe men that are successful at transitioning from their middle age role of provide and protect have the capacity to change into a coaching role. They have been there and done that, they can help without giving you the answers, and let you get there on your own timeline without getting frustrated or impatient. They find magic in seeing someone else be successful. Is that an age and stage thing, or is that a personality thing? I didn't know, maybe both...

And just like when you saw people still sporting the same hair cut for decades; they hang on because it was the best period of their life. I got it! But truly, some people knew how to grow and change—successfully transition—and some stayed in the past, and some people could keep purposefully reinventing themselves, while others got stuck. *But how do you not get stuck? How do you un-stick yourself when you feel stuck?*

I could hear the chatter of the adults at the campfire circle as I was relaxing my body down into sleep. It was our first night under an impressive blanket of five million stars. Taking a deep breath, I exhaled. I had been looking forward to *this*. A level of nothingness that I didn't even know was missing from me.

CHAPTER 6

Don't Overthink, Just Ride!

*E*arly morning arrived with a stillness that had settled the dust from the day before. Unfamiliar bird calls were the only noises I could hear chattering away. Campfire smoke and a slight foggy dampness were hanging around my stretcher-bed in a haze. Unzipping the fly of my little overnight cocoon, I caterpillared my long body towards the entrance. My feet dangled over the end to touch the dirt.

I took in my surroundings with gentle breaths. Everything in the camp was just as we had left it, but it looked different in the daylight, and I wondered what time Dad decided he couldn't continue living, couldn't face another day. Was it as the sun went down and the darkness drowned him in his own demons? Was it the crazy 3am death-hour when insomnia sends people insane? Or was it the beginning of a new day that he just couldn't face when the sun came up? I didn't know. I would never know.

I looked down at my feet. They had high arches bent like a boomerang and a few coarse manly hairs sprouting from the top of my toes. *Just like Dad's*, I thought. I shuffled around in the dirt to feel for my thongs and headed for the roadhouse loos.

After breakfast we fuelled up our long-range tanks at the roadhouse. There was a conga line of caravaners—grey nomads on their big lap of the country. While we lined up for petrol, a lady came over and spoke to Mum. She said she saw her ride into the caravan park last night, a long time after everyone else. The lady thought Mum was either a very small bloke or a teenager like me. But sitting here this morning, she noticed Mum's distinct green markings on her helmet, and she just had to come over and say that she was so proud of her. That was nice. I smiled. We were a long way from anywhere, and Mum still found herself a fan club!

There was no way any of us knew what each new day held. Gus never let on, and we just had to take it as it comes. We followed him through gates, over cross-country tracks and always popped out somewhere amazing. I'm so glad we went on this trip with a tour group. If Mum and I did this trip on our own, we would have only stuck to the main road and camped at the common roadside stops. But Gus knew everyone in this part of the country: grader divers, station owners, stockmen, everyone.

It was mid-morning and Gus had parked us at a waterfall to do some fishing while he disappeared to catch up with his old mate at the station homestead for a coffee. I didn't even see a station homestead, so God knows how long-ago Gus peeled off in a different direction. Didn't matter. Gus reappeared, swallowed down another cigarette and we were all wrestling to get our gloves and gear back on before he evaporated into the bush again.

Gunning it along on our bikes in outback Queensland was epic. Before we knew it, I could see someone up ahead stopped on the side of the track. It was Ratty. I pulled up seeing he had a flat tyre. Wasn't long before Dave came along the track behind me, Rat waved him on and then came Mum. The three of us had a drink and waited. Ralph, one of the tour guides, was always tracking somewhere at the back, not too far behind Mum. When he arrived, he told Mum to keep riding, and I followed her in case she dumped the bike on the next tricky stage. Ralph and Ratty swapped bikes so Rat could keep riding, while Ralph patched the tyre with the kit he carried. I ended up in front, and Ratty tracked behind Mum. The three of us raced in the wheel ruts and dodged our way around termite mounds. I thought it would be funny to kick a low growing mound as I rode past, but it was as hard as iron and bent my toes back in my boot and jarred my knee. I laughed to myself and paid in pain for my own stupid sense of humour for what felt like at least two hours afterwards. Eventually, the three of us came out at another road in the middle of…God only knew where!

We waited at the junction in the road for Ralph to arrive, and amazingly he wasn't too far behind. The next section of road was incredible with sandy tracks that took us down to a creek crossing where we stopped to have a snack and take a breather in the shade. This was a real test as there would be more sand further north from here. The creek at Coen was clear with a beautiful sandy bottom that looked more like a coastal waterway than something found inland. The boys walked a line through the creek to the bank of sand on the exit. Gus made Mum walk with him across the creek and pointed to the parts of the track that she should avoid.

In the normal motorbike riding hierarchy, Gus, the king, went first, he rode through and waited. Everyone else was told not to stop on the other side, just keep motoring until they were well clear of the sand. One by one, everyone got stuck. Not so much in the water, but either in the wet sand or in the deep, fluffy, white, dry sand on the exit. It wasn't a surprise when I got bogged. I stood up and crab walked my bike through with less weight on the seat while I used the throttle to drive forward. I looked back and saw Mum was down. She had dropped her bike in the second section of wet sand at the crossing. Ralph ran into the water, picked up her bike and held it steady for her to jump back on. I was still busy crab walking when Dave raced up on his bike beside me, holding his throttle hard to tackle the sand. He passed me and kept going, spraying sand everywhere. Two of the other fellas ran back to give me a hand to get enough momentum to go forward.

Mum hadn't gone far. She hit the soft white sand and her handlebars flicked out of her little fists and she was bucked off. When I glanced at the track, where I had been and she was about to go, I wondered if the motorbike pecking order should have been in reverse this time. Mum was the weakest rider with the least amount of strength and ability, yet the best riders went first and chopped up the damn track. It was stupid. My heart was hurting for her, willing her to make it. I had my hands full with my bike still stuck in the sand. That annoying emotional lump was in my throat knowing this was tough on me, but also knowing Mum had to ride the toughest ride of her life right there in that moment. I made it through and up the embankment, but I couldn't ride on knowing Mum was struggling. So, I paused on some flattened bracken on the sand at the side of the track. I looked back to see Ralph jogging to Mum's rescue, again. He picked up the bike. "Are you right, Amy?" he yelled.

"Yeah, it's just so deep and unpredictable," she replied.

Just like life, I thought.

Ralph was standing in sand, it was up over his ankles, holding the back of the bike steady so Mum could steer straight. It was the only way she was going to get any closer to the uphill exit. My heart was beating hard. Mum went about another ten metres and dumped it again where everyone else got stuck. Ralph picked the bike up for the third time and basically ran up the hill behind Mum like she was a little kid while she hung on and motored. Mum finally made it up the sandy bank exit and passed me on the track. Relieved, I thought if she could high-five me her on the way past, I would have, but I was afraid she would crash into the tree, so I just watched her go instead. I laughed a nervous but relieved laugh. My emotional throat-lump subsided, and I looked back towards the creek crossing and waited to hear Ralph start his engine. I putted along the track until I could see him rise over the embankment in my rear vision mirror, and then we raced to catch up to the rest of the riders, satisfied that we all made it!

Somewhere on the next stretch of road we travelled on bitumen for the first time in a long time, and it was a nice change for my body not to be shaken up. In my heart and mind, I felt the magnitude of complete and utter contradictions. My identity and the relationship with my dad had been constantly tossing and turning inside of me throughout this grief journey. It was like a washing machine going through every bloody cycle. I'd been soaking and spinning, clockwise and then anticlockwise for three years or more. This ride was like 'rinse and spin dry' to get that stale smell out. Jeezus, I desperately wanted to hang that mother-fucking washing out to dry. So Dad's suicide wasn't still sitting in the dirty laundry basket, waiting to be dealt with. I wanted to be brave enough to let my socks and jocks, everything, swing in the breeze on the washing line and get baked in the sunshine, and not give a fuck about it anymore.

At the top of a winding hill, the rest of our crew were waiting on a flat spot upon a ridge. Pulling my helmet off, I felt the breeze skim the sweat as it rolled down my neck, and the dirt cracking as my face contorted. My eyes cast across the treetops of deep green forest, which reached forever into the distance. Finally, as the trees tapered off, they met the bright blue sky. With the imagery of washing flapping in the breeze in my mind, I took a breath in then slowly exhaled, attempting to let go of the intensity of everything that had happened. I'm not sure if it was because I was physically exhausted, but a calming sense of insignificance as a human being overwhelmed me. I stood at the highest point on this ancient land and felt…relief.

In my helmet I was important, I was the only one there. Every decision I made had an impact. My ego could be as big as I wanted it to be. I could think through the negatives, have as many shitty sniffs, and shake my head in disgust or disapproval as much as I liked. Meanwhile, that bloody grief wombat was still trying to be digested deep down in my own serpent soul. But when I took my helmet off, I realised there was a whole world out there that wasn't swamped by grief and confusion. It was beautiful, fresh, and infinite. I felt so small in the scheme of things on the face of this earth—like nothing really mattered. If I stuffed things up, who cares; I got another chance tomorrow, and the next day, and the next. And my biggest confusion and trauma right then, was grief. Grief about Dad. But whatever Dad did, it didn't matter now—it was done. Whatever I did in the future mattered a whole lot to me, but at the same time it didn't matter at all. I was about as important as a grain of sand in this universe and my God it was a relief to get a grip on the calibre of this thing called life. Unwind that tightly coiled spring that was sending me stir crazy with worry, responsibility, sorrow. Out there, in that moment, it truly didn't matter.

Just like the steady tempo of the brake horse, I had to capture this feeling of weightlessness and relief to diffuse intensity when it became too great within me. I cast my eyes across the deep green trees on the horizon again, repeated and rehearsed that scene to replay in my heart and mind later when I wasn't out here, and needed it.

The silence was broken. Just like the winding road at the Cooktown light house, we could all hear Mum carving up the hillside. I half smiled. Bloody Mum, bringing the entertainment wherever she went!

The challenges at the creek bed earlier had knocked Mum's confidence, and I hoped a few kilometres on a sealed road would settle her a bit. I knew she'd be okay. She always was, she always would be. Mum pulled into the flat spot on the top of the hill, and I slowly walked over to her as she took her helmet off and sucked hard on her water pack she carried on her back. She spat the first mouthful out as that bit was always filthy from either dust in the straw or dust in your mouth. I asked her how many times she fell off so far today, she held up four fingers. I put my arm around her and gave her a hug. "It's a tough gig, Mum." I kissed her on the top of her head and together we walked over to the other riders standing at the edge of the lookout. Her eyes cast downwards, her confidence low, but she was doing it. We both were. I stood by her, close in proximity, knowing she needed me.

Gus casually rode over to Mum and me. He had a quick word while he sucked the life out of one more cigarette. Gus asked Mum, "How ya going, little mate?" Mum responded with a smile that covered the dirt stuck in a chalky ridge across her top teeth. She continued to sip water out of her pack as her eyes sparkled with the struggle. This ride was hitting her like a three-pronged fork; it was emotional, physical, and spiritual. Gus glanced down at his boots and flicked the ash off the end of his smoke. He looked back at Mum and simply said, "Don't overthink, Amy. Just ride…"

Back on the dirt, the next section of road included endless jump-ups. The erosion caused by wash outs were ridiculously bad. Now I understood why people travelling out here had four-wheel drives and jacked up caravans. The hard, red dirt gravel road with continuous hill after hill was like a national park maze. It was the kind of road you saw in African documentaries. At the bottom of each hill were complicated combinations of washouts that required different levels of evaluation and negotiation. After a few days riding, I was feeling the constant level of physical exertion in my core. A light-head and queasy sensation in my guts reminded me to drink more water.

Finally, the road flattened out and signs started to pop up. The township of Coen was not too far away. In baton relay style, we parked our bikes one by one out the front of the pub and went into the shade. A sign on the roof said, 'Exchange Hotel' but someone had written an 'S' in front of the sign, so it looked more like 'Sexchange Hotel', and I smiled to myself. Our crew were out the front sitting randomly at the picnic tables on their phones, it was the first place we'd had reception for a while. I walked into the bar and Mum followed. The barman, a stereotypical outback Queensland character with a big chest and deep voice asked me, "What would you like, cobber?"

"A can of coke and a packet of salt and vinegar chips, please." I wondered if I needed to add 'Sir' to the end of my reply because I felt like an underage school kid again.

Mum appeared beside me, the barman cocked his eyebrows in a sideways glance to acknowledge her, "Well, well, well," he said with surprise, "a lady rider. Let me shout you a beer!"

Mum's mouth kind of opened and then closed again in one of those moments where she had to coach herself to shut up, smile, and say, "Thank you."

Coen. Parked outside the "S-Exchange Hotel".

We sat outside where the cool breeze dried our sweat stained shirts, caught up on messages from friends and family at home, and bottomed our drinks. I was happy to be off the bike for a little while.

Everyone in this part of the country knew if you rode a yellow bike, you were with Gus. We fuelled up at the petrol station and hit the road again. We had to get moving as it was late afternoon, and we were on our way to Archer River. In a rough Gus-type of explanation, he said, "Head up the road here," nodding in the direction we would be going, then added, "and turn right when you see a rusty car-body. If you get to Archer River Roadhouse, you've gone too far." And he was gone again…

Each day of this ride was incredible. The terrain was so different. It was a test of my ability, not just as a rider but as a person. I wasn't much of a talker, a bit like Dad, but I was one hell of a thinker. Helmet time after trauma, was perfect for me.

This whole trip was about trying to settle the dust. I thought about that as I followed the red haze in front of me and wondered whether ghosts were really real. Was Dad a ghost? Was he still angry dead like when he was alive? Or was he at peace now that his struggle was over? Was that why people said 'peace be with you'? I hoped he was at peace. Mum's hippy friend had said ghosts were just unsettled energy. But was that even true? Was it me that wanted Dad to be a ghost so I could believe in something? Believe that he wasn't dead and permanently gone.

What about how we think about ghosts? Is that our own way of perceiving a dead person's energy because we want to believe a particular point of view? Damned if I knew. But while I watched the dust in front of me billow into the sky from a dozen motorbike riders, I wanted to believe Dad was okay, wherever he was. I wanted to believe my dad thought I was a good guy. I wanted him to know I was doing my best no matter what. It was like Dad was immortalised and I could romanticise this idea of him. I could turn him into anything I wanted him to be. It was a weird concept to turn a dead person into your own moral and ethical compass. It was like you're sacred once you're dead. Maybe that was just our way of being gentle about the end of life, especially an unnatural end to life.

Spotting the rusted-out car body in the distance, I started going through my gears to slow down. I took a hard right-hand turn and bumped and crashed my way over about a kilometre of consistently tough track. If Chooky and Marg were already here, I wondered how the hell the truck made it down this track. A small opening of light gave me a clue that the riverbed wasn't too far away. The square outline of the truck could be seen parked on a lop-sided angle. Everyone else's bikes had been navigated through a gravelly riverbed, followed by a narrow channel of water, and parked on a bed of boulders next to a fast-flowing river. There was no time to assess where I was going to park as I watched my front wheel drop over the edge of the track and I swung a hard left in the sand. I found a flattish, hard-ish piece of dirt where I could safely put my stand down without fear of the bike falling over, then cut my engine. I made it!

Ralph rode in front of us after we left the Coen pub. He set up his stretcher and went back up the track to lead Mum in off the road. It was likely she was going to get stuck in the washouts and wheel ruts. They were bloody horrendous!

In what had become a regular late afternoon occurrence, we were all listening for Mum to come roaring up the road. Ralph made an epic entrance on his bike going straight down the steep drop off, over the embankment, through the gravel, and through the shallow water. His knobby bike tyres rock climbed straight up the curved face of the boulders. He hit the brakes in a sudden stop when he was satisfied he'd found the best place to park.

Mum's entrance was not quite so epic. Putt, putt, putt, down the track. We were all trying not watch, but my mum was hilariously addictive. We could see the whites of her eyes as she rose to the top of the embankment before the drop off. There was no time to think about what's next in a situation like that. So, just like me, she followed her front wheel down, into the riverbed. But when Mum hit the sand at the bottom she literally went *doink* and stopped. She stalled the engine, threw her hands in the air and said, "I'm done." It was amazing she didn't fall off. We all smiled and went about what we were doing the minute before she arrived. Ralph trotted over and pushed the back of Mum's bike and her off the main track. He kicked a piece of wood under the stand and held her hand while she dismounted. Somehow, out here in the bush, when everything was filthy, dirty and difficult, a simple helping hand gesture between two people melted my heart.

And in a typical contradiction of that moment, Mum took off her helmet and said, "Fuck! How rough was that track?"

I threw my head back and laughed. A second ago she warmed my heart with how gentle and needy she was, and then she turned around and swore like a sailor.

I got her a beer and Gus walked over with me. "Are you okay, Amy?" he asked.

I relieved the pressure of the bottle top cap with a familiar *tsch* sound and handed her the beer.

She said, "Well, other than my ovaries being shaken around like two little boxes of smarties, yeah, I think I'm fine!"

It was Gus's turn. He flicked his head back and roared with laughter. I smiled. Fairdinkum! No one ever knew what my mum was going to say.

The three of us walked back to the campfire circle. Gus motioned for her to sit down in the chair next to him. "As long as you're not dehydrated, mate. It's about this stage of the ride people get a bit wobbly."

Mum took off her boots and emptied out the water from this morning's water crossing. She peeled off her long pink and purple socks, her feet all white and wrinkled just like mine.

Gus kept talking, "Your boy has made your bed already." Gus winked at me in approval.

Mum sipped her beer, patted me on the knee and replied, "Awesome! Thank you, I'm the luckiest mummy around."

CHAPTER 7

Unicorn

A couple of dozen big, fat lamb chops sizzled on the hot plate. The open fire glowed orange and red, reflecting on the familiar faces sitting around our camp. Margy arrived with a handful of plastic shot glasses and cracked open a bottle of coffee tequila. She'd been hiding it for a special occasion, and today was a celebration that no one broke their neck! I swallowed down my tequila, the liquid warming me from the inside out.

Conversations were bubbling, freely flowing just like the Archer River behind us. Ratty sat between Mum and I. Sharing todays ride made us mates, so it wasn't uncomfortable when Ratty asked, "So, where is Mr Olsen, Amy?"

I thought about how often people have a piece of information about someone else, and it turns into gossip. It pleased me that no one here talked about us, about our circumstances.

Dirt and Dust

Mum was as gentle as she could be, and replied, "He died, mate."

Ratty's mouth dropped open a little bit. He took a couple of seconds to compose himself. "Oh, jeez, I'm sorry. So, that makes you a… widow. It's just that, you're too young to be—" He looked at Mum differently, kind of squinting, like he had a bad taste in his mouth.

Mum cut him off, "—It's okay." Just like me, she knew how the conversation would go—that stupid guessing game with the three questions all over again.

There was a pause from Ratty while we all took a sip from our post tequila drinks. Mum was on the lemonades; she didn't want to be any more dehydrated tomorrow after Gus' warning about being wobbly. And Mum knew that in the morning she had to ride back up that two-boxes-of-smarties, ovary-shaking track she just rode down!

Ratty spoke first, "Must be hard to lose someone you love."

Mum did one of those small, tight-lipped smiles again. "Yeah, it's complicated though, mate. Suicide is a head and heart minefield. It was messy in the end. I knew it was likely. I was waiting, hoping it wouldn't happen."

There was a big pause as all three of us digested that thought. Ratty spoke, "Jesus, that's no way to live, Amy."

Mum nodded. "But what do you do when you are so in tune with the other person's moods—their attitude, their everything—but they hate you for helping? You've loved them better and begged them for change, moved away from your friends and family, and supported them to do whatever they needed to do to stay alive." The three of us stared into the crackling fire.

Ratty's face squinted as he filled in the gaps, thinking about why Mum and I were riding to the tip of the country. He spoke again, "Are you going to burn your wedding dress at the top? Chuck your wedding album off the cliff? I'm not sure I'd know how else to deal with it."

Mum used her non-emotional voice—I'm not sure if the tequila had steadied her or whether four days riding knocked the edge off her ability to be upset about it anymore. Either way, she was calm and rational—and said, "Nah, you don't understand, Ratty. I didn't hate the guy. I loved him."

I know it was shocking and awkward, but to tell you the truth, I respected the hell out of Ratty for being fired up about suicide being so awfully wrong. When you looked at my mum, my sister and me, we appeared like we were holding our lives together. The three of us were strong. Some time had passed, so it wasn't so raw. But there was always this cloud, a shadow of darkness that sneaks in on even the brightest of days, just to remind us that things were...damaged. Ratty was clearly a passionate man, he was wrestling with the confusion of it all. He looked Mum in the eye and said, "Amy, I hope you don't feel like a failure."

Mum took a moment to think about that. My eyes flicked from Ratty, to Mum, to the fire, and back to Mum as she spoke. She confirmed the answer to his question. "Mmm...failure that my marriage ended, yes. Failure that my husband died, yes." We all cast our eyes down, and then she broke the silence that hung heavy in the air. Her tone was steady but positive, and in almost a whisper she said, "But what is the opposite of failure? I kept my husband alive for fifteen years. It's just that no one knew the struggle, mate. That was our business, no one else's. If I talked about it, he thought that was me undermining him..."

The push-pull of Mum and Dad's circumstances were evident in that statement right there. Love, hate. Right, wrong. Failure, success. Win, lose. Whatever. This wasn't a bloody game. There were no sides in this. It was our life story, it included each of our individual lives. But she did it, Mum successfully did it. She turned it around, she did the one-eighty degree turn and turned that dirty, big, negative motherfucker of 'failure' into a positive. And I knew 'failure' of the end of their marriage and loss of Dad's life would have come freakin' faster if she hadn't tried so bloody hard.

In defence of Mum's role in all of this, Ratty spat out the words, "Yeah, but you are left carrying the guilt that he killed himself."

Mum's mouth moved uncomfortably. "Yeah, that's true. It's heavy, mate. But do you know what? I also know, deep in my soul, there was nothing left on the face of the earth for me to try…to help him…" Mum's voice trailed off before she added, "It kind of felt inevitable, mate. It wasn't a matter of *if* he killed himself, it was *when* and *where* he was going to do it."

Ratty looked at me and then at Mum square in the eyes and shook his head. "It's still not fair though."

"I thought it was in my head Rat. I thought I was imagining how bad the situation was. I'd see his behaviour starting to escalate and I'd often suspect he was suicidal, even when he didn't mention it. I'd mentally start preparing. Every time, I hoped I was wrong. And it's an awful thing when your intuition is right. When you've spent fifteen years trying to love, encourage, and save someone. Then spend eight months holding your breath when they stop talking to you and you don't even know where they live. Then eventually accepting that he did it, after all of that time. De-compressing, that's been hard. That's been my biggest hurdle. Trying not to be so anxious because my own intuition scares the shit out of me. It's awful when you are right about something that is so fucking wrong."

Ratty leaned forward on his camping chair, held his beer between his hands while his forearms leaned on his knees, taking in everything Mum said. He looked sad, disappointed. He finally spoke, "I just don't get it, mate, you're a beautiful little family, you've got a daughter as well, the man was the luckiest bloke alive."

Mum shrugged an 'I don't get it either' answer in response. There were no words that could change the outcome or help anyone understand it better. The more I tried, the more questions I had, not answers.

Chooky was mashing potatoes in a giant silver pot. His arms manually pumped up and down and I thought about how my Dad was a chef before he was a farmer. But the dad I mostly remembered was the one that worked away in the mines. Chooky double-banged the side of the saucepan and loudly announced dinner was ready.

Crikey, those chops were good! Chooky even remembered to pack mint jelly in the tuck-truck fridge. It was a perfect gourmet dinner under the stars out here in the middle of nowhere.

I chewed my chop bones and threw them one by one into the fire as I listened to the conversations around me. Rat asked Mum, "What the hell went wrong, Amy? Why did it turn bad?"

"I don't know, mate. Expectations."

"What do you mean? They didn't match up?"

"Yeah. I remember when the kids were little, we had a farm in Victoria. I used to get really upset with how he would speak to me. One day he yelled at me because I couldn't tell him why I was so upset. When he kept pushing me for a response, I finally said, 'You expect me to work like your dad, cook like your mum, and fuck like a whore. That is fine, you can have all three, but not on the same day!'"

Ratty's mouth dropped open in surprise, then he held his guts and laughed, hard.

Mum finished it with another famous smile, "He didn't speak to me for about three days."

Ratty smiled in return at the thought of my feisty little mum throwing verbal punches when she was hurting. It was kind of cruel, but a fight is still a fight.

Mum softened after her smile, took a sip of her drink and said, "And then we'd make love and turn the corner again, and be okay for another three or six months without too much trouble."

Nodding, Ratty knew that familiar relationship cycle—love, fight, love.

Mum asked him, "What about you, Ratty? What's your story? I'm sick to death of mine, literally."

"Oh look, it just sounds pathetic. We've got two little boys. I'm trying to do all the right things, but it's difficult."

"Hmm," Mum responded.

Ratty's face was screwed up in emotional pain. "I'm just really angry. Angry I tried my guts out and it still didn't work."

It was Mum's turn to nod and listen. She let out another thoughtful 'mmm' in response and then added, "I hate it when that happens, mate. Some partners use the children as pawns. God, it upsets me. Those children need to know they were a product of *love*, not the *problem* between their mum and dad."

Ratty paused and stared blankly at Mum. Like she hit a raw nerve with him.

Mum leaned forward on her camping chair, closer to the fire. She corkscrewed her can of drink into the sand next to the leg of her chair and turned her hands backwards and forwards in front of the fire. "Ratty," she said, "the only thing you can do, is not play the game, mate." He looked at her sideways. She continued, "Don't say anything negative about your kid's mum. Don't disapprove of anything. Just accept that when it's your turn to have them for the day or the weekend, you need to make sure it is the best damned day, every single time. It's not about bribery or entertaining them. It's about loving those kids and allowing them to trust every word you say, and every action you take. Including every little thing towards their mother. You don't need to be a doormat, but don't get caught in the petty fighting, mate. I guarantee, by the time they are eight and ten they will know everything they ever need to know, trusting their own judgement, about both you and their mum."

Ratty didn't say a word, but I could see his eyes blinking as he was thinking.

Mum left it for a few minutes, and then she pulled one of her swiftie conversational moves to change the subject. "So, what's this bullshit about female orgasms are like unicorns, anyway?"

I burst back into the conversation. "Jeezus, Mum!" It was the first thing I'd said since dinner!

Ratty's mouth dropped open as he stared at Mum, clearly mortified.

It was Mum's turn to push the conversation, "Well? I'm pretty sure it was you that brought it up."

Oh my God, I was trying to stall for time here so Ratty could compose himself for some kind of reasonable adult response. Stating the obvious, I butted in, "Subtle as a sledgehammer, Mum."

Ratty hung his head in shame and embarrassment. He looked sideways at Mum through the corner of his eye, testing the water. "I didn't realise you heard that…"

"The walls are thin, Ratty." Mum laughed. "But I can tell you this, women who know their body and know themselves don't fake orgasms!"

She smiled wide and sincerely but convincingly drilled a hole into Ratty's level of understanding about a woman's world, "It takes trust and time. And there is nothing more special than a lady who feels safe and loved enough to desire a man. And when she does, she'll *invite* him to enjoy her mind, her spirit, her body and it will *blow your freakin' mind*."

I had to think about those words. Let them sink in. Trust. Time. Desire. Invite. Mind. Spirit. Body. Ratty would have to be at least ten years older than me and ten years younger than Mum. His face just stared aghast beside the campfire. I was too embarrassed to even move my eyes sideways to see who was going to speak next.

There was a big pause before Ratty replied, "Jeezus, Amy, you're the unicorn."

Mum shook her head. "No, mate. There's nothing special about me. As soon as you 'unicorn' someone it paralyses them. You have to love the humanness of people, mate, not a fantasy."

This conversation was bizarre, like my mum was the first woman to walk on the moon. I'd never heard those words before.

After a long pause, Ratty finally said something, "Your husband had the whole deal, mate, I can't believe he gave up on that."

Mum looked down shamefully at her tattered looking toenail polish that was chipped and rough after being knocked around in her boots for four days.

"Did he try to get help, you know, for himself?"

"Yeah, but he didn't take it seriously, mate. People have to choose to make a change. He still wasn't owning the behaviour or the outcomes. When he died, the coroner's report identified antidepressants in his blood and obvious consumption of alcohol. It was just so mixed up in the end. I kept compromising to save him, but it was an inevitable disaster."

"What about his family? Are they good with you?"

"I thought we'd be grieving for the same person, but it didn't turn out like that. At the exact moment I was telling the kids that their dad died, I received a text message, it said, 'You're such a bitch, Amelia, it's all your fault.'"

Ratty was gobsmacked.

Mum's face grimaced. She always got red and flustered about that. "Maybe it was a shock response, an initial reaction. I mean, I get it,

I understand. Everyone wants to blame someone. Okay, fair enough, it's me, but that's been my biggest struggle…coping with the blame, knowing I did my best to keep him alive for a really long time, only to be punished for what I *knew was* likely to happen."

Margy interrupted the intensity of the conversation as she came around to offer each of us small squares of dark chocolate on the opened foil wrapper. She truly was the mum to all of us on our trip. It was a nice, thoughtful surprise. *How do mums know to do that? Forward plan a gesture like that?* I said thank you and popped two small squares of chocolate into my mouth. Ratty kept the questions rolling.

"So, what did you do about a funeral?"

"We just had a private cremation. Just me and the kids. I asked the funeral director to express post my husband's ashes to my mother-in-law so he could be there in time for his own memorial service. But they had to resize his casket three times, so it didn't quite turn out as I had hoped. Honestly, I didn't know what else to do. But if I was the mum in this scenario, and my son took his own life, I'd want my son back, I'd want the final say. That was the kindest thing I could think of to do."

Ratty stared into the glowing coals of the campfire, "Jeezus, that was generous Amy."

"Yeah." Mum sighed and took in a deep breath. "But what else do you do?"

I took a sip from my can of beer that was rapidly getting warm and chimed in with a big wide hand gesture towards the fire, "Ride to the top of the country, to let it *all* go."

CHAPTER 8

Wingman

It was early morning. Everything the sun touched turned to silver. The rocks, the twisted and knotted roots of the trees in the riverbed, everything. Mum was out of her stretcher before me this morning. I took the camping shovel and went for a walk. By the time I got back, Mum was looking as fresh as a daisy and dressed in her riding gear. She must have had a wash in the water beyond the boulders downstream. Last night, I overheard Margy telling Mum to hang her pink towel in the tree as a signal to the boys to stay away because it was her bath time in the rock pool. I smiled at the thought of a shared secret kind of girl scout language between the women on a boys' trip.

Two giant black kettles were boiling on the hot plate above the campfire. Someone must have been up before Mum to get the fire perfect in time for breakfast. I felt doughy this morning; maybe I had too much beer and a touch of dehydration. Mum didn't have a cuppa this morning, but she had a fizzy orange flavoured Berocca in a camping cup and made one for me too.

Today was the day we were going to tackle the Old Telegraph Track. Three-hundred-and-fifty kilometres of narrow, rough, rocky, sandy track. It was four-wheel drive only. Unless you are on two wheels, then of course, it's two-wheel drive, only!

After breakfast we packed our own lunches, and Gus explained the plan of attack for today's ride. "Righto you blokes, and Amy, listen up." He winked at Mum. Gus kneeled down in the riverbed with a stick and drew a rough map in the sand. "When we get out of here, stop at the Archer River Roadhouse and we'll fuel up there. It's only about five kilometres. Amy, we'll all stick together for a while, do a few little tricky spots, but after the Bramwell Junction Roadhouse, you'll ride up the road by yourself. We'll come off the track and meet you at lunchtime. You right with that?" Gus looked up at Mum. She nodded in return.

Gus continued with his stick drawing. "Then there are three sections of the track that we are going out on. I'll take you blokes up the track, but if it's too rough, I'll send some of you up the road. It's the first ride of the season, so I'll be able to gauge the condition of the track in the first few K's. No guarantees, we've had a massive wet season."

Gus stood up and said, "Saddle up fellas, it's going to be an excellent day."

Ratty walked back to the bikes with Mum and me. "Are you disappointed that you're not doing the Telly track, Amy? It's what I've waited for. It's iconic."

Mum smiled an enormous smile. "Not at all, mate. My goal was Cape York. I've still got three solid days of riding to get there. Anything more than that is a bonus! I can't believe I've made it this far."

Ratty smiled back at Mum. "Right attitude, Amy!"

Engines revved, and one by one each rider disappeared up the embankment that we all rode down yesterday. I had to have my mongrel-attitude on in the first five seconds of today's ride to get the hell out of that gritty sand in the riverbed. There was no gentle motoring up the highway to ease into today's ride!

Riley. Archer River Roadhouse.

We had a quick stop at Archer River Roadhouse. I had just enough time to guzzle a chocolate milk while we re-fuelled our bikes, then we were out to the middle of nowhere again. I'm not sure how we found ourselves in open, grassy country, followed by a range of extraordinary washouts, but we did. On the road we could be spread out like a rubber band over kilometres, but where it was tricky turns and troublesome terrain, we were all bunched back up together. It was just as well, because sometimes it took four blokes to pluck a bike out when it was bogged.

Riding mid-pack, I was starting to get my confidence up. I was in awe of how much I had improved as a rider this week, until we headed down a track towards Lockhart River—there had been a few wash outs, but this particular one was a cracker. Gus, Doug, Shane, Chance, Chase, and Ratty had all ridden through and were waiting on the other side. As I rode the rough as guts creek bed, I could see another major drop off below. I couldn't even explain how complicated this one was. All I could imagine was a broken leg coming right up. This cut out in the road was like a big dipper in a roller coaster ride. The bottom section was missing and there was only a narrow strip about a foot wide to ride across. I didn't want to pause for too long on the entry before I lost my nerve, so I kicked the bike into second gear and rode forward. I made it down and across the missing section, and then up the other side with just enough momentum. My back tyre got stuck between a rut and a horizontal tree root just before I made it clear of the creek embankment on the high side.

Ratty and Chase were already off their bikes. They were running back to help me before I toppled off the embankment and into the dry riverbed, more than a metre below. With one bloke on one side and one on the other, still astride my bike, I put my feet down and revved my throttle. The back wheel of my bike spun, spraying dirt in what Mum referred to as a rooster tail! With both Chase and Ratty in the creek bed cut out, the two men pushed my foot pegs upwards. They lifted my back wheel out of the rut where it was spinning and digging a deeper hole.

My adrenaline raced as I was finally able to ride forward. I parked beside a big tree where Chance was waiting for the other riders to come through. Next, we heard Dave's engine travelling down the track. Chance said, "Hell knows how Dad's going to do that." And just as he finished speaking, Dave headed to the right of the track and went bush bashing to make his own way through. We all watched sixty-two-year-old Dave, unsure if he was doing the right thing. It looked messy, like he was going to get caught in a trap. He was in a tangle of trees and vines, and on unsteady ground while he navigated his own way in unchartered territory. It's funny how you barrack for people in your heart and mind, willing someone on when you see them in their struggle. It is silent. Almost a secret that you want them to be successful.

It took a bit longer, but it was the smarter option for Dave. He made it up the embankment and cut his engine. Chance gave his dad a big smile. The three of us sat there, poised on our bikes, sucking on our water as we waited to hear Mum bouncing her way down the rough track. I couldn't help myself, but I repeated what Chance just said, "*Hell* knows how my *Mum* is going to do that." We were all holding our breath and smirked at the same time.

Cartoon character Mum made it to the top of the embankment, her body looked tiny sitting on that big yellow bike. Chase and Ratty were still waiting in the bottom of the creek bed. I wasn't even sure Mum had enough skill to line the bike up accurately, position her front tyre to make it onto what was essentially the tight rope of a ride across the only remaining part of the track. The bottom of the crossing had fallen away, a section was missing, and I'd just dug a bigger rut next to the tree root where my tyre got stuck. At least I had long enough legs to stand up and stop the bike from toppling over, Mum didn't. For the first time, Mum looked like she didn't think she could do this. As she sat there looking at the combination obstacle, nervously, she pulled her left glove and then her right glove tighter onto her fingers and refastened the Velcro. She looked to the right where Dave flattened the bush on his way through, then looked back at the two men waiting in the ditch. Ratty shook his head to say, 'No, don't go that way.' Mum started talking in motorbike sign language while she sat still on her bike. She pointed to Ratty, and role played, 'Will you ride my bike through?'

Ratty shook his head in a definite, 'No.'

Mum pointed to Chase and asked him the same thing.

Chase shook his head in a definite, 'No.'

Mum looked up at the sky. I wondered if she was praying. She wasn't a religious person, but maybe if you are desperate enough, anything is worth a go!

Mum's eyes cast over the creek bed again. Ratty held up a single finger to tell her to go in first gear, and then he twisted his wrist in a motion to tell her that she needed to seriously throttle it. Chase turned his body side on to Mum, pointed with two gloved fingers at his goggled eyes, then pointed to the tree on the exit next to where Chance and I were waiting. Chase then double-tapped under his chin and pointed back at the tree as if to say, 'Look up and aim for the tree.'

My heart was in my throat and I was so anxious. It was almost like I didn't want to watch. I didn't want to watch my Mum make a mess of it. I didn't want to see her fail. I didn't want to know this was the point where she would likely break her neck.

Mum kicked the bike into gear and revved her motor hard. She lined up the foot-wide tight rope dirt crossing, skipped the missing piece at the bottom of the drop off, jumped the horizontal root I got stuck on, swerved in the sand to miss the tree on the exit, and then motored like hell without looking back!

I couldn't believe it; she rode it like a textbook professional. I let out a whoop of relief and excitement before laughing so hard and chasing her down the track. It was so unbelievable, I almost cried.

One by one we all overtook Mum on the track. She didn't care because she was riding, not racing, and she was still smiling from ear to ear when we pulled in to Bramwell Junction Roadhouse. At the halfway point between the east and west coasts of the Cape York Peninsula, we had enough time for an ice cream and a can of drink. Not long after we arrived, Chooky and Marg left again in the truck, as they would be going slower than the rest of us. Mum waited for the dust to settle before following them up the main road. Meanwhile, the rest of us boys followed Gus toward one of the most talked about tracks in the country.

The Telly Track was sandy, like riding on another planet. The track was rough and had been carved up by four-wheel drive tyres. To negotiate water wash outs and craters while you are astride a motorbike literally sitting on an inch of rubber was amazing. It was incredible that none of us had broken any bones, already.

We met up for lunch on the side of a river, and I was calculating the risks of the next unknown section of the track in my head. *Do I feed my own ego at the expense and likelihood of coming a gutser on this track?* I was only pretty fresh at this motorbike riding thing, and I still had a couple of days riding to get to the top of the country! With that in mind, I said, "Mum, I'll ride with you up the road from here." She would never have asked me to do that, but I knew she was grateful.

Just like me, I think Dave must have been making the same simultaneous equations. In his gentle Dad voice, Dave said, "I'll be riding with you from here on, Amy." Mum nodded her second enthusiastic smile in the same number of minutes. Now there would be three of us going up the corrugated red dirt highway.

Gus's instructions were always classically simple, "Head up the road until you see a sign that says 'Ranger Station' and wait there for the truck. Should be about twelve kilometres on the sand. When you get there, pop in and say g'day to the ranger. Tell him you are going down the track to meet up with the rest of us. Amy, ask him if you can park your bike in the bushes, tell him you'll be back in the morning to get it, then hitch a ride with Chooky and Marg in the truck. We'll see you at the camp!"

One by one we filed out onto the highway. Chooky and Marg parked at the exit to let us riders go in front of the truck. Dave rode out first, in his steady confident style. Followed by Mum, still a bloody beginner who had more luck than ability, then me.

From when I was about eight years old, Mum had always said I was her right-hand-man, her wingman. If she wanted anything done, she'd ask me to help her. Together, me and Mum could do anything. Then it occurred to me, maybe that is exactly what made Dad jealous of our relationship. What he didn't realise was, it was his attitude that *forced* Mum to rely on me.

I rode behind Mum, flanking her to the right. Close enough for her to see me in her mirror, but far enough away so I didn't cop her dust. I held a constant throttle grip at one-hundred kilometres an hour, and I didn't think I was pushing her with the speed. Maybe that was my role in this suicide bullshit; be her wingman. Not push, but hold steady while she navigates her own way, and I navigate mine.

We headed down the orange, sandy track. I stood up on my foot pegs to look over the low-lying bushes on either side of the track, taking in my surroundings—the vastness of this place was amazing. I promptly sat my arse back down again when my back tyre slipped and slid in the unpredictable sand.

The three of us riders slowed down as we neared the ranger station. Ralph overtook us to do the early introductions and ask if Mum could leave her bike in the bushes for a sleepover.

Little Number 8 bike parked in the bushes at the ranger station.

When Ralph was about four, he lived at Heathlands as his dad was the park ranger at that time. Ralph had a stickybeak around to relive memories from when he was a little tacker, while the bearded fifty-something-year-old ranger chatted to us.

"Amy, let me shake your hand." Mum smiled and put her hand out and wondered what this was all about. He continued, "You're smart enough to listen to the advice given to you. Right now, it's four o'clock." He pointed to his watch on his hairy right wrist and looked skywards to see where the sun was. "Do you know how many times I've had to call a helicopter at five on a Friday afternoon, all because someone on a motorbike has broken their neck down there at the crossing? Fairdinkum! Riders are tired, dehydrated and they have no idea how to tackle it. Now, hop in that truck, and I'll happily see you in one piece in the morning!" With that, Mum smiled and said 'thank you,' then climbed in between Chooky and Marg to enjoy the last few kilometres to camp.

We regrouped at the river crossing. Ralph put his stand down and walked into the flowing water that was up over his knees. Both Gus and the ranger had given him the heads up on how to ride the crossing. Chooky, Marg and Mum went first in the truck. Chooky had seen this crossing a few times, so he knew how to negotiate it, but it was still pretty daring. The recent wet season had changed everything, and although it may have looked familiar to Chooky, he assured us it was different every time.

Ralph, Dave, and I watched the truck traverse the crossing. It crashed its way under low-lying branches. Bumped its way through the rocks beneath the rushing river water. Turned at a complete-right-angle and travelled on what looked like a rock shelf parallel to the river before meeting up with the track that required a sharp left-hand turn.

The exit track was grey, slippery sand and silt, and this is what the ranger warned us about—the break-neck corner. Water was draining from the bottom of the truck as it travelled up the slope making the track slippery, giving us bike riders an extra thrill. But me, Dave and Ralphie made it. At a small widening of the track, we overtook the truck and took off to meet the other riders at the secluded camping spot.

When we got there, smiles were broad. Everyone looked really pleased with themselves. The three of us fronted up to the gun riders who also met their very own level of challenges on the last section of the track. It didn't take long before our camp was set up and the boys went fishing. I swam in the fast-flowing river while Mum and Margy had a glass of white wine and dangled their feet in the river.

CHAPTER 9

Flowers Can't Fix That

Margy started the conversation, "What a day, Amy!"

"Yeah, when we came down towards the river in the truck I was thinking, what is the ranger talking about? Then we made it through the other side, and I saw the grey silt on the exit. I was really glad to be in the truck with you."

Both women chuckled at the level of complexity and sheer strength that was required to cross the river with the water rushing through the crossing. Margy continued, "I used to ride, not this type of riding, I had a road bike up until about three years ago. After I broke my elbow and was turning sixty, I decided it was time to let Dave do the riding and I would be pillion and photographer!"

"Oh wow, that's cool."

A glance of mutual respect was shared between the women who were separated by a twenty-year age difference.

"The boys have told me how rough it is out there, Amy, so I think you are doing an amazing job."

"You know, anyone can say that Margy, but coming from a lady that can ride means a lot."

There was a reflective pause in the conversation between the two women.

"Amy, how the hell did you get to this point? Where you take on something so ridiculously big like this ride?"

Mum glanced over at me. I was still rolling about in the cool river water, trying not to appear to eavesdrop on the girly conversation. Mum smiled her dare-devil smile. "There is ten-percent of me that is *crazy*, Margy. I don't honestly know how to settle all of the emotions in my soul, and I want to finish the things we started."

"When did you know that things could be…difficult, with your husband?"

"The first time I *really* thought I could be in danger was when Riley was a three-month-old baby. We'd only been married for six weeks. We were kind of jobless and travelling around the countryside in our little car. We towed a trailer and lived in a tent. We were somewhere out past the Devils Marbles in The Territory. Riley was crying, I didn't know why. Whether he was hot or tired or was just sick of being in the car seat. I asked my husband, 'Can you just pull over?' He ignored me, turned the radio up and kept driving. I was more assertive the second time and said, 'You need to pull over!' He did.

He pulled a long way off the side of the road, but he didn't get out of the car, he didn't turn and look at me. When I got Riley out and closed the door, he drove off. Innocent me thought, 'He's probably going to park the car and get set up for lunch. He's probably just going to turn the car around.' Nope. He left me there with no hat, water, or wallet. I had a screaming baby that was going blue, Riley was crying so hard…"

Margy stared at Mum in disbelief. "He drove away? Amelia, the man was insane!"

"Yeah, the dust just billowed up into the sky as I watched the car and trailer disappear. I was puffing little breaths into Riley's mouth to get him to take a breath. I was jiggling him and bouncing him trying to get him to stop crying so hard. Eventually, I crouched down in the dirt so he could breastfeed. Riley's little body was still letting out a sob or taking in a big breath every now and again. I just looked at him and thought, 'It's you and me kiddo.'"

"What the hell, Amelia? Did he come back?"

"Yeah. Took a while. I was just making up my mind what I was going to do next—walk back to the highway, don't get bitten by a snake, catch whatever vehicle was going south—and then he came back, told me to get in the car. I honestly didn't know if I wanted to, I just said, 'Don't ever do that to me again.' Took me until the kids were teenagers to even mention that incident. But you know the stupid part? I felt lucky. Lucky that he left. I didn't end up with a shaken baby syndrome scenario. But I realised, when he was like that, it was always about him not coping, so I took care of everything. That was my way of making sure there were no bad outcomes. I just did it, no matter what needed to be done."

Margy stared at Mum. "You're a survivor, Amy!"

Mum did the shitty sniff in response. "Sometimes you don't get a choice, mate."

"Do you think suicide is a selfish act?" Margy asked.

"Sometimes. Sometimes when I see my kids missing their dad I think, 'you selfish bastard, why couldn't you wait until they were ready to see you, on their terms?' But then maybe he thought he was so fucked up that the kids were better off without him."

The two women had a sip and continued to sit at the edge of the river.

Mum spoke again, "I also understand on a mental health level, when people are stuck in their own negative thoughts. Or they are chemically depressed in their mind and body, or they are in enormous physical pain. Or tragedy is so great in their own heart and mind, I get why they would end their life. I wholeheartedly understand. But then it's just magnified for everyone else, and God it hurts."

"How do you fight it, Amy? Fight those frustrating thoughts?"

"It's really difficult. I don't hate him, but jeez it's tough sometimes. He was so fragile, but in contrast, I had to be absolutely bullet-proof. Somehow, I have to accept that in the end he made an adult decision, which by default has made me the sole guardian of our children, his legacy and their future."

Margy nodded, "That's not going to be easy, Amy."

Mum nodded a slow 'yes' in return.

The two women looked at each other. Margy questioned, "Everyone probably asks you this, but did he leave a note?"

"Yeah, but it was empty, hollow. It actually made me really angry. Was that the best he could do at the end of his life? Maybe I'm an arsehole for thinking that."

"Was it addressed to you, specifically?"

"No. It was very broad, only a couple of lines. But I knew he would have been angry to end his life. Every time he did something that required determination, he was angry. The piece of paper had a tear up the middle of it, like he tore it out in anger." Mum paused again, and then added, "It makes me want to vomit, replaying that scene in my head. I know exactly how he would have moved, what his eyes would have looked like, his attitude, everything." Mum spoke through her clenched teeth, "For God's sake, the whole situation is painful and ridiculous."

"How do you survive the grief of losing your husband when love is conflicted with anger? When the disappointment is overwhelming?"

Mum was shaking her head. "It's not something anyone can really comprehend. I joke that sometimes I'd like to take Valium, or I need a treadmill in the loungeroom for night-time running. The 3am insomnia is crazy."

Sipping her wine, Margy let out a little chuckle, "I'm just creating a mental image of you pounding the rubber belt of a treadmill. Endless kilometres in the loungeroom at three in the morning! You're hilarious, Amy!"

Shrugging, Mum added, "When I'm in a tough spot, I listen to music or run around the block. I throw myself into jobs that need to be done." Mum laughed, my smirk revealed that I'd been listening to their conversation. I laughed too because I'd seen Mum do it; turn the stereo up flat out and scrub the stairs or shovel trailer loads of mulch. Jobs that burn energy and cause physical exhaustion to put that nervous and angry energy somewhere positive to take the sting out.

Mum paused, looked at the rim of her wine glass and then looked at the older woman sitting next to her. "Umm, it's weird, but strangely enough, I don't drink much. I mean I could, but any more than two drinks and I'm a hopeless, crying mess. It's like I can't let myself. Circumstances didn't allow me to relax and let my hair down in my marriage. Somehow, in the back of my mind, I knew I always had to be able to run, fight, save, bloody-well drive to the hospital, I don't know, literally sleep with one eye open."

"Did something happen for you to be like that? Or was it just living with someone who was anxious?"

Mum replied, "Both. There are so many things, Margy, and I was young. I was trying to figure out what part of this behaviour was him struggling and what was just shitty attitude. I don't know, but somehow, I became a pawn in my own life story. I don't think it was intentional by him, but I was constantly walking this kind of metaphorical tight rope, weighing up whether it was the right time to address whatever the issue was, or leave it alone because it was…just going to be bad."

The two women sipped and sat there. Despite the heavy conversation, I was happy to be still basking in the contrast between the river's flow and the rough ride we had just tackled. Mum spoke, "My loyalty paralysed me. I didn't want to upset him because I knew the outcome could be life or death. So I just coped the best way I could; keep my mouth shut and work hard. I managed whatever was in front of me to the best of my ability, managed the kids around him, and tried not to put any pressure on or create any conflict."

"I can see why you did that, Amy. You wanted to keep your family together."

"Of course, I did. And every time I started to tell him what I saw, what I thought, what I needed him to do about it, he just took that as if he wasn't good enough, that I would trade him in. It's like he didn't believe I loved him, and I made a commitment to him, to us, to our family and our relationship."

"Did he threaten suicide?"

Here it comes again. I could see Mum's face clearly as she spoke, "Yeah, it was directly stated at least half a dozen times. It was genuine. The problem was, I lived it ten times as frequently as he did. I was watching his behaviour and felt I was more aware than he was. If he was out of sight and gone down the farm too long, or if the machinery took too long to turn on in the dairy, I'd start to prepare myself. Pull my boots on to check, go and see if everything was okay. It was a bullshit existence, waiting, hoping my intuition was wrong."

Margy let out a slow breath. "Dreadful…"

"It was our normal, Margy. And then it's awful to think that a death message about your husband brought a sense of relief. I felt like I had done my job as a mum and wife because our kids didn't have to find their dad. I know that is fucking terrible. God, I felt bad about that, I still do. But it was my biggest fear for a really long time. I was a nervous wreck. I'd conditioned myself to find him, identify his body if someone else found him. All of that anticipation for years and years. Hoping I was wrong. But when he died, I hated being right. All those times I checked and waited. I was ready to run and save him. Finally, I was deflated with relief, exhausted from holding my breath."

Mum broke down and cried. Margy didn't say anything. What could you say? Absolutely nothing.

"You did your job, Amy. You loved a man, and he didn't know how much, but it was unfair to expect you to keep trying."

Mum talked through her tears, "I'm so determined not to be a victim in this situation, Margy. Sometimes, I accidentally come out fighting. I'm not a bitch fighter, I'm just overly assertive. It's probably a result of regret, me not standing up sooner in my own circumstances. I don't know, but I feel like I've ended up with a sixth sense for suicide. If I identify that someone might be on edge, I keep checking on them. And it's the same thing if I think they have mysteriously backed away, I think I'm looking for a body. In my mind I think if anyone needs to find them, it should be me, like I've prepared myself for it and I don't want anyone else to do the dirty work."

"Hmm, did you ever get any help, you know, to help you cope with him not coping?"

"Do you know what? I've thought about this a lot. Maybe that's what I *should* have done. *I* should have got counselling. And if I went first, maybe he would have accepted that it was okay. Maybe an indirect approach rather than a direct approach would have been better, softer, more acceptable to him."

"Maybe, Amy, but you can't convince anyone of anything. You can lead a horse to water, but you can't make it drink."

"I freakin' know. I would have even drunk it for him if I had to. That's just me, mate. I didn't want this shitty outcome, not for him, me, us, our little family, even his own freakin' mother."

Margy's calm and steady voice spoke, "I can see that, Amy. There's nothing you wouldn't do to help anyone. But people must help themselves, especially grown men, you can't *make* them do anything, they have to *want* to."

Mum's face grimaced in half a smile. She looked over at me. I stood up out of the water and I responded with, "Must be time for me to grab a beer, I reckon, Mummies." I climbed up the riverbank, grabbed my towel that was hanging in the nearest gum tree and playfully flicked it at them on my way past.

Sipping my drink, I sat at the campfire behind the two mummies. I could still hear their chatter. There was a break in the conversation before Mum started again, "It's so confusing though, Margy. I loved what we had. I loved our little family. I loved how hard he worked. I loved it when he was my gentle giant. There were things that happened that made me stay, made me love him harder when he was struggling, made me be the reliable, unflappable one, you know? So, he could get his feet on the ground, again."

"Yeah, it's hard. When you love someone, of course you stay. You don't want to see them struggle, and you sure as hell don't leave them when they're like that."

"I don't want to blame anyone for anything, I own my part in this. I knew he would likely kill himself, but after years and years of the same stuff, and it was getting worse, there was nothing left for me to do. I honestly think he couldn't re-engage with people because he was hurting too much. It was loneliness, paranoia, and insecurity that killed him. He needed the language to communicate, but he didn't, he couldn't."

Mum's face was hard with hurt for a few moments, she looked around at the trees that were moving above the river. "I tried to reconnect with his mum just recently. It's been a few years. Honestly, I was as gentle as I could be. I didn't want her to hate me and take that to her grave. I tried to speak with her face to face, I offered the olive branch of hope, friendship and reconciliation, that's the best I could do. I just thought we'd be grieving for the same person…. It didn't work out. Never mind. I got told in no uncertain terms that she didn't want to have anything to do with me. I had to walk away and leave it. I tried. It wasn't easy. But it's done."

"How the hell do you deal with that?" Margy asked with her eyes squinted as if concentrating that hard helped to understand better.

Mum took a big breath in and let it out slowly through her mouth. Sighing was a real clue that emotions were heavy inside of her. That was the deep stuff. "It's taken a long time to get it right in my head, Margy. But in my heart of hearts, I know I tried my hardest for my husband and again with his mum. I know I tolerated things when he wasn't right, and he wasn't coping. I know no one works harder, stays longer or loves more than me. When he smashed up the house, he sent flowers to my work. I hadn't told my boss what was going on, but we live in a small town, so people knew. The principal of my school simply said, 'Flowers can't fix that, Amelia'. And I knew I couldn't continue to tolerate it anymore, no matter what the reasons were, mental health or not. My kids needed to know that it's not okay to accept that kind of behaviour in a partnership. The shittiest part was, I knew he could end his life at any time when I said, 'no more'."

Margy's face did an upside-down smile to acknowledge those words. Mum did her uncomfortable kind of fidget on the spot, swished her legs in the river a few times and thought about what she wanted to say next.

"I think everything can be okay in your conscience when you know your intentions are true and real. People are always going to misinterpret your actions, your words, sometimes deliberately. People can only understand from their own level of experience, their perception, and that's okay. I believe the universe is a witness to everything, to the person that you are. Maybe that's me trying to understand integrity and keep myself in check. And I have to trust that other people have good intentions. If I believe that, I know I'm safe and I can be brave. And if that isn't true, I have to be strong enough to stand up and speak the truth. It's as simple as 'no, I disagree for these reasons …'. That's it, that's all I have to do, and the rest is on them. And if other people are offended by what I say or how I conduct myself, I know that if our souls' cross paths into the future, I've still told the truth. I've still done my best, and I've tried to understand their point of view."

"That's a fantastic philosophy, Amy."

"I don't want this situation about suicide or our circumstances to make me bitter and twisted. We've lived in a world of anxiety for so long, and I don't want to be old before my time. We all need hardcore happiness and the capacity to build hope for the future; that's soul work. I have to do this ride, try to settle the dust. Stop shadow boxing this stupid invisible ghost of grief."

The two mums moved slowly and steadily back towards the camp in time for dinner. Tonight, there was a seafood entrée compliments of the fishermen among our crew. They caught a few local cherabin which looked like freshwater prawns delicately placed on the BBQ plate next to some little fillets of fresh fish.

Margy cracked open the tequila between entrée and main and that burning black liquid got swallowed down quick. She filled up Mum's shot glass for a second go, "You're safe, Amy. I think you need two dashes tonight!" The women smiled at each other and downed the second nip. "Cheers!" relayed around the campfire like a Mexican wave. There were a few of us that knew today was a lucky, unbroken-neck kind of day.

Cherabin and fresh fish!

CHAPTER 10

Knots in Jocks!

Morning came. Mum had already bathed and was shaving her legs in the fast-flowing river.

"Jeez, Mum, do you have to?" I asked.

We both laughed and Mum replied with, "I know it's rough out here, but that doesn't mean I have to be completely feral."

Our crew enjoyed another beautiful breakfast in the bush. After lining up our bikes to refuel from the bowser on the side of the truck, Mum hauled herself up onto the step and shuffled in between Chooky and Margy. Our breakaway group of riders headed back the way we came last night to collect Mum's bike. As we left the camp, Ralph pulled an epic mono in an expression of excitement for another day of adventure.

Mum's little, lowered Number 8 bike was waiting right where she left it at the ranger station. Chooky fuelled it up and she climbed back in the saddle, ready for more moon racing on the sand back towards the red, dirt highway. There were no other words, but this place was amazing.

Heathlands National Park.

For the second day in a row, I was Mum's wingman. We took it in turns for me to lead when she was tired, or she'd jump in front and I'd track behind her. I didn't pay attention to the distance we travelled, but there seemed like endless kilometres spent standing on my foot pegs and skipping across the top of corrugations at one-hundred kilometres an hour. It was incredible to look out beyond my front tyre and see absolutely nothing but red dirt. Low growing green shrubs bordered each side of the road, and fluffy white, flat-bottomed clouds in the sky directed me along the path like beacons on an airport runway, leading me towards the top of the country. My core felt strong, my centre of gravity was low and confident, yet my heart felt light and my head clear. I knew this was the right way to say goodbye to my motorbike riding dad.

My mind started to wander to when Mum was teaching me how to drive a car. It didn't take long before I got the feel of where the gears were, and I wasn't crunching them or bunny hopping the clutch down the road anymore. At sixteen years of age, I thought every gear change was a racing-change. I was flooring the car in second gear, revving its engine and driving it hard until Mum said, "Hey, when you get your own car, you can drive it like a mule, but when you're driving mine, you drive it like a Mercedes, okay?" Well, that didn't mean much to a boy who had never driven a Mercedes, so her next trick was to tell me, "You need to drive like I'm sitting here with a full schooner of beer in each hand, and you don't want to spill a drop." We both laughed. It made me a better driver, well, at least when Mum was around.

I caught up to Dave on the road, and the three of us were bunched up behind a caravan going slow. Dave eventually overtook, and I let him create a reasonable distance between us, so I wasn't choking on his dust in the haze.

Settling into the rhythm of the road, I felt like I was on autopilot today. Either deliriously dehydrated or just at peace in myself because I was going steady on the bike, chewing up the kilometres and so far, today, there had been no big challenges.

Back in my helmet headspace, I thought about people. How they spoke, the way they talked about things. Whether they were superficial and full of horseshit. Whether they had standard, well-rehearsed-one-liner come backs, ones that they were not emotionally attached to. Or whether they were really in-depth conversationalists and meant every word that they spoke. Or were they listeners and observers, like me? I wondered about how people move their bodies and how their voices were a reflection of their personality. I wondered if people with monotone voices were also monotone lovers. I smirked to myself and thought about me, my voice, my movement, and how eighteen-year-old me will develop into twenty-five-year-old me, then into forty-two-year-old me, like my dad.

I thought about Mum's four friends who she affectionately refers to as, 'The Bullshit Radar'. One cop, one teacher, one truck driver and one farmer who moonlights as our little country town's first responder. Luckily for us, Mum knew how to pick good people. Ones that were kind and clever, had enough grunt. Normal everyday people. And in that period where it was really messy after she had to ask Dad to leave and Mum didn't know what to do, she could ask anyone in the bullshit radar for their opinion or their help and trust their judgement when she didn't trust her own.

I thought about my uncle, Sam. Mum rang him first when she was told about Dad passing away. Sam picked up Grandma and they drove for two days from Melbourne to be with us. He literally walked in the gate at ten o'clock at night and said, "What do you want me to do?"

Mum cried and said, "I don't even know yet."

I realised my imagination filled the gaps where there was missing information, especially when I was in the process of trying to make sense of everything. Just like when Mum and Uncle Sam went to the place where Dad ended his own life; Sam raced around the house, literally looking for skeletons in the closet. Unnatural death does strange things to people. Even when you know that particular person isn't there, but it's like you don't want to face any more danger, you don't want any more dreadful surprises. We all have that sense of responsibility—me, Mum, Sam, even my little sister—that sense of doing the dirty work so no one else has to.

In another 'sit-down-this-is-important' moment at the dining room table with Mum, she told us exactly how things were when her and Sam got to the house where Dad lived, died. She told us straight, "I don't want you to imagine things to be worse than they actually are…" The conversation that followed, essentially went 'this is what we found, this is what we saw, and this is what we did.' Facts. She told us facts to settle our souls and our curiosity. At any time in the future, we could go back to the facts. Facts allow things to be pure and real in the dirtiest of circumstances. Then Mum shared how grateful she was to have her brother there to help her fold up the bedsheets just like when they were little kids, move the furniture, tidy up the kitchen, pack Dad's things into boxes, take the rubbish out. That part was all very normal, very natural after such an unnatural event. But the good thing was there was no need for my mind to create any bad stuff. There was no room for doubt. The facts with no gory details were told to me as if I was there, seeing everything for myself.

I thought about the stupid court case Mum had to go to months after Dad died. The owner of the house where Dad lived tried to charge her with a water bill for seven thousand dollars. I couldn't believe people could be so callous. Trying to take a dead man's money was the lowest of the low.

At that thought, I recognised another shitty sniff had just escaped my nostrils and I shook my helmeted head in disbelief. And it was true, someone dying isn't the worst thing to happen, it's how people behave when they do.

My mind conjured up a cartoon image of my two grandmothers' facing up to each other at the memorial service for my dad. One accusing the other of creating a situation where one of their adult children tragically took their own life. *Fuck, does it get any worse?* Both women defending their own child. Meanwhile, more than a thousand kilometres away, those two adult children were in a funeral parlour with the children they made from a union of love, saying their final goodbyes.

The dust was hanging in the air like a thick, magic screen from whoever was on the road in front of me. It was my opportunity to practice my one-eighty-degree brain flip, to train myself to look for the good. I thought about how people could be fucking amazing. People who hardly knew us literally crossed the street to hug Mum, tell her they heard the news about Dad and ask if there was anything they could do to help. It was incredible to live in a small country town with a community like that. If we lived in the city, someone could die four doors down and you wouldn't even know.

Gus's timing on this section of the track was impeccable. Just as us road-riders were turning right into Fruit Bat Falls for our lunchtime stop, the Telly Track riders filed into the car park.

Our lunches were in my backpack. Mum and I dismounted our bikes and headed towards the walkway. The track opened and so did my eyes when the falls presented themselves in front of us. The landscape out here was flat, so the water was spilling over a wide shelf with a drop off about two metres deep. The constant volume spread over such an incredible natural shelf, pouring into an enormous pool of crystal-clear water below was impressive. While our riding crew was peeling their motorbike gear off to climb into the water, Mum rolled her eyes and said, "I wish someone told me today was the day I needed to pack swimmers. I didn't come all of this way just to watch. Look the other way fellas, I'm going in!"

We slipped down the side of the rocks and into the cool water and swam across to the rocky outcrop above and clung to the rocks as the water cascaded over us. If ever there was a water cleansing ritual, this was it. Baptised at Fruit Bat Falls; wash away the bad, soak in the good, and capture the very best of what mother nature had to offer.

The elastic on my jocks were shot, and the water weighed them down. I had a good laugh with Mum about tying a knot in my boxers to hold them up. "Hey Riley, you got your knickers in a knot!" she laughed and swallowed water giggling on the swim back across the pool to our starting place. We took our time. Swim, float, swim. I wouldn't have cared if this was the final destination of our trip, it was magnificent. Reluctantly, we hauled our bodies back out of the rock pool and shimmied our clothes back on. Still soggy yet squeaky clean, we sat with our legs dangling over the edge of the rockpool and ate our sandwiches.

The rest of our crew were getting ready to move, and that was our silent cue to do the same. I took a big breath in as I scanned the waterfall and committed the scene before me to memory. My mind was photographing everything in front of me with all my senses. At some time in the future, I would need to recreate this place for my night-time meditation when sleep was hard to find. I stored it for when I needed thoughts of beautiful places to relax my body and mind. This was a location that could transcend time and place. I rehearsed the thoughts of what I had just experienced…floating on my back, belly button pointing skywards, the sprinkling of water misting on the exposed front surface of my body, my face, my chest. My feet flip flopping gently in slow motion to keep me suspended in the full relaxed

The annoying little knot I tied in my jocks to hold them up!

stretch of my own body. Warm sun on my skin. Water sealing my submerged ears so that every sound was dull except for the constant cascade of water to bring me back to the present moment. I thought about the annoying little knot I tied in my jocks to hold them up, it was digging into my hip, but I didn't care. I smiled at that small slice of humour. This was peace.

Amy. Fruit Bat Falls.

Looking over at Mum biting into an apple, I wondered if she was doing the same as me, literally soaking this place up in her own steady silence. It occurred to me that you didn't have to be stone cold dead to find peace. Peace was in experiencing beauty, like I just did. It was an hour of my life that would be replayed in my mind over and over again. One hour of living to sustain life in the darkest and dirtiest of moments. I needed to collect them. I needed to collect more just like that.

We rode out of the car park in a single file just as we had ridden in. My body was relaxed, my mind at peace. Me, Mum and Dave, up the road we went, nearing the Jardine River. Gus' morning instructions were to wait there until Chooky and Marg arrived in the truck, then cross on the ferry together. We sat and had an ice-cream from the shop

Amy and Riley. Fruit Bat Falls.

at the caravan park, and I found a scorpion to play with in the dirt. Pointing to the creature, I said, "Hey look, Mum, it's you!" I stroked it with a stick and chuckled, "Tail up means don't mess with me!"

Mum replied, "Look at me, I was harmless until you poked me with the stick, son."

Dave chimed in, "Every mum is like that, Riley." And the three of us grinned and ate our quickly melting ice-creams.

The river flowed fast, and the ferry looked like a flat decked platform with a ramp on the entry and exit. On our trip, there was enough room for the truck, our bikes, and a ute before it had to track back to the other side of the riverbank for the next load of traffic. As the ferry bumped the bank and the boom gate was

Jardine River Ferry.

lifted, we started our engines, and I took the lead up the ramp and back onto the red dust.

Next stop, Seisia, where we would camp the night and ride to the tip of the country tomorrow.

After nearly thirty years on tour in the Gulf of Carpentaria, Gus had his favourite designated camping places. As we rode into the park, I wondered if crocodiles wandered up onto the sand in these parts that overlooked the Torres Strait. Somehow, I didn't think my little stretcher bed would be much protection against the chomping teeth of a prehistoric monster in the middle of the night.

The three of us were ahead of the main group of riders and helped set up the camp. When the rest of the boys rolled in, it was tequila time—Margy was like Mary-fucking-Poppins with that medicine at the end of the day. It took away the pain of any busted-up knees or elbows that copped a flogging on the ride. We headed down to the beach, each of us with a frosty beer in hand to sit on the sand and watch the sunset. I caught a shitty sniff and supressed it before it snuck out. The sunset was hazy, was I disappointed? I imagined it was going to be magnificent, especially when we had ridden all of this way. Sipping my beer, I leaned back, relaxing in the sand on one elbow. Maybe it was supposed to be like that, not perfect, just raw and real and unexpected. Maybe the sunset tonight was better than I could have ever anticipated. It came down to how I looked at it, how I interpreted it.

After dinner there was a pause in the conversation and I heard Margy ask Mum, "I know we are not there yet, but I've been thinking about how you've planned this trip for six years, and after tomorrow it's done, that's it. I…umm…I don't want you to fall in a heap when you get home. I suppose I want you to have an idea of what's next for you."

Flames from the fire flickered and reflected on the faces of the two women. Mum nodded in response to Margy's question, taking a careful minute, then responded, "Well, I don't have to ride motorbikes anymore."

They both laughed and sipped their drinks. "This is the *start* of your riding career, Amy. You look comfortable on that bike, and I don't know how someone with as little experience as you got this far."

Mum smiled. "I don't want to speak too soon, but I'm amazed I haven't been carried out of here in a helicopter. Seriously, I was prepared to break every bone in my body and get skinned alive to finish this ride."

"I know," and Margy responded with a laugh.

"I…umm…I've decided this is the last time I'll do anything for my husband. But I will do things for mental health. I work with high school kids, and I just think if my husband had better strategies as a teenager, things could have been different."

Marg nodded. "I don't really want you to be a public speaker on this suicide crusade, Amy, it's too draining. You've got the rest of your life to live, without sadness, without the trauma of it all."

"I agree, but I feel like I have to contribute *something* through this life experience."

"I'm sure whatever you decide will be just right. Amy, you don't do things by halves," Marg smiled at Mum.

"Yeah, I think I also need to rehearse a cover story."

"What do you mean?"

"Well, it's just that when I meet new people, I'm tired of my own story, conversations are often sad or awkward when you are in my scenario. So, I think if I rehearse what I'm going to say I can keep the conversation going. I can make it positive and polite and then I don't have to answer all of the dead husband questions. I reckon if I say, 'Hi my name is Amy, I'm the mother of two awesome teenagers, I'm a teacher and I did this amazing ride to Cape York on a motorbike!' I reckon that will keep me out of trouble, initially, anyway."

Mum smiled a big cheeky smile of satisfaction and Marg's eyes sparkled in response.

Margy stared at the flames in front of her. "Amy, I hope love comes your way. You deserve it." It was like the older lady was giving my mum permission to let someone in to share her life, so she could love and be loved again.

Swallowing hard with tears sparkling in her eyes, Mum's response was a whisper, "Thank you. I do feel lucky though, Margy, lucky that I have loved. Some people never get to experience love like I have. We made a family from love. I just have to remember that. Be grateful for my husband's contribution, graceful about what all of this has taught me. Remember why I loved him, remember all of the good. As the kids grow up and eventually leave home, I think the hardest part is being the sole keeper of the good stories. They are not shared with anyone else."

Mum's voice broke my own thought process, she turned and was talking to me now instead of Margy. "Do you know what I think I've figured out on this trip? I think I fall in love with difficult things. I've wondered why I wrestle with stuff other people don't even think twice about, they can just end things and move on. But for me, unless there's some kind of resolution, I just don't give up. I probably make things a hundred times harder by being like that. Just like this ride, it was unfinished business. I promised your dad we'd do it. It was the goal, the *thing* to look forward to. I don't know if he didn't believe hard enough in the dream, the goal, or whether he underestimated my commitment, to him, to us, to complete the things we said we would."

I nodded in reply. "I know, Mum."

"Sometimes I think I struggle because I've got a romantic view of the world, I believe in the good. Good things happen, good people exist.

I'm not romantic as in make-believe fantasy, I just think I'm romantic in the way that I'm looking for good, aspirational outcomes. The difference is, I'm prepared to work for it, it's like I wrestle with it until it's in a comfortable place in my soul. I can live in a bubble of love and hope when I have the romantic perspective because I'm looking for the good in everything. But when that crashes, I'm fucking hopeless."

"But that's also why you are loveable, Mum. We can see the struggle, we can see you try."

Mum smirked. We both knew that feeling—a constant internal cyclone of being heartbroken, pissed off, blamed, but not letting it beat us. Then add a generous dash of love and purpose to whatever cause we decided to throw ourselves at. Some people didn't know how to identify their own emotional cyclone. At that thought, Mum blew a shitty sniff out of her nose.

"What was that Mum?"

"What?"

I pointed to my two nostrils with my fingers in a motion of air coming out of them. "You just made this little, puff out of your nose, like a backwards sniff, you did a shitty sniff, like Dad."

"I don't know, I was just thinking about what you said."

"It kind of went like this—" and I mimicked Mum with a single shitty sniff.

Mum did two shitty sniffs in return. We both laughed. "Must be bedtime. Night, mate," she said as she kissed me on the temple and headed beyond the light of the campfire towards her stretcher, hiding in the bush.

CHAPTER 11

Top!

It was the last day, and the camp seemed like a place of mourning. My face was pale, and I felt a bit queasy in my guts. Anxious. We were close to the finish but hadn't quite made it. I was exhausted, yet I didn't want the ride to be over. I didn't have the words and thoughts ready in my heart and mind to say goodbye to my dad.

On our ride into the town of Seisia yesterday, there were road signs to warn of wild horses in this part of the world. Somewhere between the smoky campfire and the beach, a curious mare and foal were circling. Mum got close enough to pat the mare, maybe because Mum was steady and quiet. Maybe it was her confession yesterday about falling in love with difficult things. The mare and foal skittered away when Ralph was banging and crashing around in the back of the truck, looking for cooking utensils to give Chooky a morning off from breakfast duties.

As Mum walked back towards me at the campfire, she smiled wide with satisfaction that she successfully patted the horses. Life was a dare to my mum, and at the same time she was so bloody ordinary. I snapped a photo of her on my phone and glanced at the picture on my screen. Yep, she looked just like everyone else's forty-year-old mum; ordinary. Ordinarily awesome. Maybe Dad dying drew attention to us, to her, to me. Otherwise, we would still be that stereotypical white, middle-class family of four. Mum was a teacher, Dad was a miner, one son, and one daughter. The usual photos of family holidays, Christmas, birthdays, school events; our life looked just the same as everyone else's. It almost grated on my nerves that Dad ruined it. We had what everyone wanted. I still didn't get it; I wasn't sure if I ever would.

Mum and I had roles to play in these circumstances. But my little sister was the anomaly in this whole fucked-up scenario. She just loved Dad, and Dad loved her. She was Dad's girl, and that should have been a big enough reason for someone—anyone—to live. Was Dad just greedy? Was it a personality thing? Was it his own hurt and abandonment that got projected onto the rest of us? I don't know.

When Dad died, I was fifteen, for God's sake. I was eighteen now, and people say things like, "Make sure you look after your mum and sister, okay?" I don't mind comments like that, but Mum did. I would nod and she would do a covered teeth smile, but I knew it secretly pissed her off. People thought that was the right thing to say. But it was like stating the obvious—of course I was going to look after my mum and sister.

But Mum knew for years that she was preparing to provide the stability for us that Dad couldn't. She accepted everything he had to offer, and respected and valued his contribution, but knew one day it could all be over. She deliberately chose a job with a steady week-to-week income. She knew she had to have her bases covered, whether Dad was around or not.

I loved my dad, but it was complicated. I knew he was hard on me—most men were tough on their sons, I got that—but then there was simply being unreasonable. I didn't know then my emotions were being shaped by the impact of my dad's behaviour. My emotional responses had to fit between 'not too happy' and 'not too sad'. If I was too happy, he would be jealous. If I was too sad, he'd think I was ungrateful. I just learnt to operate somewhere in the middle.

I asked myself all the time; if Dad was so difficult, why am I sad? I was sad because he couldn't love me for who I was. I was like him, but I was also *not* like him. I was the same, but different. I was a different person and that should have been okay with him. I wondered if it was drug-damage on his own developing brain that capped Dad's emotional capacity to comprehend that being different was okay. In fact, being different was a good thing.

On funeral day, our farewell with Dad had already been delayed by a few days. The undertaker rang Mum to tell her that they had to get a casket specially made for Dad as he was too big and didn't fit anything they had. My response wasn't a shitty sniff, it was half a scoff and laugh. In those careful questions about caring for dead people, the funeral director asked Mum what she wanted Dad to be dressed in. Jeez, how did you even answer that? He tactfully suggested a shroud, a white silk suit like short legged pyjamas. I smirked at the thought, Dad didn't wear pyjamas.

In preparation for us going to the funeral home, Mum asked my sister and I if there was anything we would like to send with Dad on his final journey. Jacinta made him a cake. It wasn't a celebration cake; it was a cake of kindness because food was the biggest thing our little family of four shared. She cut him a slice and wrapped it in a gesture of thirteen-year-old girl innocence with love for her daddy and left it on the lid of his coffin. That day, we stood there, the three of us and Dad. A simple wreath of flowers, natives, just like Mum's wedding bouquet, were carefully placed on top of his enormous casket.

Mum held our hands. Eventually, as her hand was shaking, she reached out and touched the cold, metal, oval plate with dad's name and age inscribed on it. She shook her head in disbelief. We stood there, each of us holding our own private conversations with Dad in silence. Other than us, the only thing in that room was a few chairs up against a wall.

After what seemed like an eternity, Mum walked away from Dad and sat down. Tears poured like sheets of rain down a windscreen. There was no point trying to wipe them away, it was like she knew the windscreen wipers wouldn't work, so there was no effort to even attempt to turn them on. She didn't sob, her face was still, frozen with grief and disbelief.

And Jacinta was like a deer in the headlights. If you loved people, you didn't need to fucking kill yourself.

We are not better off without you, Dad. You could have been alive and still been a part of the family you created. I don't hate you, but I am dirty that you couldn't even give time or effort to my sister. You can hate Mum for standing up to you, you can be hard on me for whatever reason you want to imagine, but you treated her differently. What happens when she has a shitty boyfriend? Me or Mum have to sort that out. And you missed all the good stuff. Like when she gets married. Or she has a baby. You told her you loved her, but you still didn't stay, Dad. And who is going to sharpen the carving knives to cut Christmas roast, or buy Mum a new nighty for her birthday, or watch us graduate from high school? Fuckin' who, Dad? You bloody well just gave it away…

Snapping back to my thoughts in the present, sitting in a camping chair at the fire, my right leg started to do that stupid anxious uncontrollable shake. When I wanted to run and there was no reason to, my body had no way of letting out my nervous energy, I would notice my leg start to pump up and down. I was getting too angry in my own head again. Hastily, I got up and walked over to the toilets behind our camp area. Sitting in silence in the cubical, I had to recompose myself. Today was supposed to be about being gentle and letting go, and all I had done was get fucking wound up and angry.

With my pants down around my ankles, I stared at the family of slimy green tree frogs that were behind the door. They looked fat and slippery, happily stacked on top of each other. Feeling suspiciously like I was being watched, out of the corner of my eye, I caught a glimpse of something and turned my head slowly to look upwards. On the divide between the cubicles was a curled-up carpet snake. My heart rate went up. I waited. It wasn't moving, it was completely still and quiet. With one eye on the reptile in the rafters, I steadily pulled my pants up, gently flushed, and backed my way out of there. It was my turn to look like my very own cartoon character in a comedy.

I left the building that was up on stilts and washed my hands in the outdoor sink. Mum was on her way over to the ladies' loos. *Should I say anything? I'd better.* "Hey Mum, umm, just have a look up before you sit down in there, okay?" I smiled. She already had her scorpion ponytail in place. Mum looked at me like I was playing a trick on her. She didn't say anything, but gingerly opened the door. She looked up, paused, registered that a snake was coiled in the rafters between the cubicles, and went in.

We met back at the campfire and looked out towards the sandy beach in front of us, Mum spoke first. "That snake."

I looked at her sideways and waited for her to continue.

"I think it's time for it to shed its skin, mate," she said.

No words were needed, my anger had subsided, as I nodded in reply. She was right. It had been nearly three years since Dad died. Saturation from suicide was toxic. I couldn't afford to question the 'why' of Dad's death anymore. I couldn't afford to be angry or upset because I would ruin my own life, my own relationships, my own everything…everything.

Ralph was cracking a dozen eggs into little metal rings on the hot plate above the fire. I stared at them. I hated eggs; I'd always hated eggs. They were those weird little chicken bum-nuts. Why would you eat them? But the bizarre thing was, they looked like the perfect image of happiness, right there on the hot plate. Bright, yellow suns surrounded by an orbit of white having their arses cooked off by the fire below. Ralph called out to his breakfast audience, "Who's having their eggs sunny side up?"

Silently answering in my own head, 'Sure as hell not me!' The breakfast parade travelled past the hot plate to collect their bacon and eggs, but at that moment I realised it truly was a choice to stay sunny side up, even when your arse was being cooked.

Gus was kind of like Mum in the way he never really asked anyone to help, he just got started and then people jumped in. You never want to disappoint a person that was self-motivated. They knew they could do things themselves, but it was like you were a magnet, compelled to join in, because you wanted to. Maybe that was how Gus managed to do these tours for thirty years, maybe that was why Mum wasn't your stereotypical schoolteacher.

Motorbike chains were being checked and oiled. I was grateful for the predictable, familiar manual routine tasks I knew I was capable of-they stopped the anxious leg shaking that kept creeping up on me. I needed to be busy doing stuff to settle my nerves.

Ralph was helping Mum oil her chain and I snapped another picture of her. Ralph moved on to the next bike, the rider leant their bike over on the stand and spun the wheel.

"What are you thinking about, Mum?" I asked.

"Your dad."

"Me too. What about, Dad?"

"Just how he had his priorities all mixed up. He bailed too early. It's like he didn't believe me…that we could do this trip, or even that I loved him enough to keep trying."

"I know, Mum. I kind of feel…empty. But I'm so glad we're doing this trip."

"Yeah, mate, me too. I've decided I'm drawing a line in the sand after this. Stop the feelings of guilt creeping in when I'm happy. Stop feeling sorry for him."

"I get it, Mum."

"You know, Paddy said to me one day that you can't be controlled from the grave, and he's right."

I nodded and thought about that, 'controlled from the grave', is that what happens? I supposed it was if you let it, and maybe that was why the rest of us had to live our best lives. It was okay for Mum to try her guts out to keep Dad on the rails when he was alive, but now that he wasn't, it took a whole different mindset. Instead of being anxious and ready, Mum needed to put it down, we all did, and accept that it was Dad's final decision, irrational or not.

Mum spoke again, "Your dad and I weren't divorced, but somehow I feel like I have to make a formal psychological divorce, and divorce being a widow. Step away from it. I know it won't make a rat's arse of a difference, but this ride is my way of doing that. With as much gratitude and grace as I can muster, it's in my heart and mind that I have to make a definite distinction."

"It's okay, Mum, you have to live your life for you, not for Dad. You fell in love with him a long time ago. I know you'll always love him, somewhere, somehow."

Mum nodded and there was a pause in our conversation while we pulled our jackets on and prepared to ride. Mum quickly scooted back to the ladies' loos for a nervous wee. Doug rolled his silent motorbike up next to mine and asked, "How ya goin', mate?"

"Pretty good, thanks," I replied, looking at him, scanning his face for a clue as to what was going to come next.

"Keep the sun on your back today, mate." And he double patted me with his big, open palm fair and square between my shoulder blades, right where I was supposed to feel it. Doug was sharing a timeless secret with me, one that would keep me warm on the darkest of days, for the rest of eternity.

I sat astride my bike, letting the words sink in. *Keep the sun on your back.* I nodded a thank you in acknowledgment towards Doug and pulled my helmet on. Mum trotted back towards us and mounted her bike. She climbed on board and bloody well hit her horn instead of the ignition button, again. My head flopped backwards, my eyes looked skywards, and I groaned at her either geniously timed humour or short memory that the start button was on the other side. *Bloody left handers*. My hilariously hopeless mum.

Engines roared with confidence as we filed out of the caravan park.

It wasn't all that far from our base camp to the top of the country. We stopped at a few places along the way and finally put our stands down in the car park to wait for Gus and the other boys who had ridden up the beach. Mum, Dave, Ralph, and I were enjoying the scenery where the mangroves were low, and the palm trees were high. The tide was out, exposing the wet sand on the beach. Aqua coloured water gently lapped the shores of white sand on the most northern beach in the country.

As Chooky and Marg arrived, a low hanging branch became snagged on the windscreen wipers of the truck. Chooky's long arm reached out of the open window, he grabbed the branch from the windscreen. The truck was still creeping along slowly past Mum who was standing in the carpark. Chooky held out the two-foot-long stem with all of the grace of prince charming of the northern peninsular. His voice called out to Mum, "Here, Happy Mother's Day, Amy!"

Mum made three giant strides towards the door of the truck and took the stem from Chooky. It was a spontaneous gesture of kindness, and I smiled with surprise as Mum's eyes sparkled with tears. "Thank you, kind sir!" she said, laughing, "I love it." She placed her hand on her own chest where the emotion grabbed her heart. She did a little girl curtsey complete in dirty, smelly weeklong motorbike clothes and big boots with her face still covered in red dust. Everyone who was a witness to that moment smiled.

Our crew congregated at the carpark in preparation for the climb to the sign at the top of the country. We all carried a drink of whatever we wanted to celebrate with when we made it. I didn't pay too much attention to who was where, I just knew Mum was at the back, taking her time.

It was like I didn't believe we had made it. Mum walked down the natural amphitheatre towards the rest of us at the sign marking the tip of Cape York. She carefully climbed down the rocky outcrop, soaking everything in. The wind swirled around each of us, water crashed against the rocks, sea spray hit our lips and cooled our skin. It was almost like I felt this scene more by watching her. As she got closer, Mum smiled an enormous smile, I smiled back. We hugged. I felt her body let out a sob. I was so proud, of me, of her, and of us. "This is it, Mum."

Everyone shook hands, our crew all hugged Mum. We sipped our drinks and took in the surroundings. Mum and I cracked open our cans and clashed them together. I offered words of a toast towards the sky, "To Dad."

And Mum replied with her words for Dad towards the sea, "Peace be with you, my big man." And we drank.

We posed for a photograph in front of the sign. Gus surprised everyone by spraying champagne all over us in a celebration of accomplishment, and I opened my mouth to catch the bubbles. There where whoops and cheers from the bunch of people who were all strangers a week ago. Gus passed the bottle around and we all had a drink. Mum was the last, she held the bottle in her left hand and took a sip of champagne, then raised the can of Jack Daniels in her right hand for Dad. We posed for a photo with the men who helped us make this dream become a reality. Eventually, I moved and sat a short distance away on the rocks that faced to the north and watched as Mum and Margy had a girls' moment at the sign.

Margy thoughtfully said, "It's your turn to live and love now, Amy, you are free to go."

The two women hugged, and Mum's body deflated as her tears trickled out.

It was a steady, but satisfied and sombre climb back down the rocks to our bikes that were waiting in the car park. We rode back from the tip to the eastern side of the peninsula, and to tell you the truth, it was the best riding Mum had done all tour. Like the weight of the world had lifted off her. Was it the fact that she deliberately let Dad go at the top of the country? Or was it one beer, one Jack Daniels and a slug of champagne that made her as ballsy as hell and bullet proof on the bike?

The tide was out so there was plenty of sand to play on. Us boys raced our bikes and pulled monos for the whole length of the beach. After some free time and one last photo opportunity with our whole crew lined up, we parked our bikes and headed in the direction of campfire smoke and the beckoning smell of barbequed sausages and onions.

We resumed our usual places in the chairs around the lunchtime campfire circle. My eyes cast toward the beach and I wondered what Gus was doing. He was riding his bike slowly along the edge of the sand, standing on his foot pegs and scanning his eyes along the tufts of grass that cap the edge between the sand and where the cliffs start to climb. He looked like he had lost something.

After Chooky announced that lunch was ready, my fellow riders and I ate and stared at the campfire smoke in disbelief that our ride was complete. As Mum grabbed a couple of cans of soft drink from the esky in the back of the truck, Gus appeared. His shirt was all rolled up in front of him like he was a big kid hiding a precious bounty. He smiled at Mum and unravelled the shirt. Gus grinned and held out an enormous perfectly formed pearl white nautilus shell. "Congratulations, Amy, you made it." Mum held her hand up to her mouth and gasped at the gift from nature.

We all felt Mum's knees go weak in a wave of overwhelming emotion. How did you ever say 'it's over' when you'd spent your whole married life hanging on, loving someone and willing them to stay alive, saving them from themselves? The shell from Gus was like a giant, beautiful, smooth full-stop in the gritty dirt and dust love story of my mum and dad.

Was this it? Was this ride the ultimate act of triumph over tragedy? Riding to the top of the country to finish the family wish list, challenging yourself to complete a crazy goal in order to create some kind of closure? And was this really the end?

But maybe this was the beginning for Mum, and the beginning for me.

I thought about how frequently snakes popped up in our journey, and wondered how many transformative skins each of them would have in their lifetime. How many would I have? And are shed-able skins even countable in this crazy cycle called life? Because where the hell do they start? And where the hell do they end?

My heart hurt. But again, there were no tears from me.

I looked around at this special place and thought about my dad. It occurred to me, maybe he left this lifetime prematurely to make room for us to enjoy our own individual levels of freedom. Maybe he thought suicide was the ultimate selfless act. Maybe that was my heart trying to tell my head to be grateful, gentle and gracious in such a savage set of circumstances. Maybe, like Mum, I needed to stop questioning. I needed to shut up and just smile no matter how much it hurt in my heart. I needed to say, 'thank you' and get the fuck on with the rest of life. I didn't know. For whatever reason, I had to accept that Dad made his own final decision. No one made him do it. No one took his life away.

It's not that Dad didn't choose me, or Mum or my sister.

He simply didn't choose life.

Riley – At the top of the country!

About the author

Amelia Olsen
Amelia is a schoolteacher working in Queensland and studying for a PhD. She has two children.

Riley Olsen
Riley, the narrator of 'Dirt and Dust' is a qualified mechanic and currently working on a cattle property in the Northern Territory.

Jacinta Olsen
Jacinta, Amelia's youngest, is living and working in Northern Queensland.

Contact details:
Website: ameliaolsen.com.au
Facebook: Amelia Olsen
Instagram: dirt.anddust
Instagram: ameliaolsenauthor

Cape York – It's a bloody long way!

Acknowledgements

To our family and friends. We are sorry it's been such a shit-show, but forever grateful you stuck by us, no matter what.

Photo credit and a million thank yous to Damien Ashenhurst for the fantastic front cover photograph!

If you need help or assistance relating to the issues raised in this book, the following organisations may be of help to you:

Lifeline	13 11 14
Men's helpline	1300 789 978
Suicide Call Back Service	1300 659 467
1800 Respect	1800 737 732

www.beyondblue.org.au
www.blackdoginstitute.org.au
www.blackdogride.org.au
www.headspace.org.au

Notes

www.ingramcontent.com/pod-product-compliance
Lightning Source LLC
Chambersburg PA
CBHW021151080526
44588CB00008B/297